Praise for *STOP YOUR C(*

"We tend to think that complaining isn't a particularly serious sin. After all, everyone does it! We complain about the weather, our sports teams and how long we have to wait in line at the grocery store. But Martin shows us that complaining is a deadly serious sin, and he points to the biblical path for change. Don't let complaining conquer you. Read this book!"

—Stephen Altrogge
Author of *Untamable God* and
The Greener Grass Conspiracy

"If complaining is a cancer, Ronnie Martin comes to us with the only medicine strong enough to help us find deep and lasting contentment: the gospel of Jesus. If you fight this heart condition like I do, this book will be a great help to your soul and your joy."

—Matt Boswell
Pastor of Ministries and Worship and
Director of Doxology & Theology Providence Church

"Ronnie Martin surgically removes the sinful cataract of complaint and once again gives us eyes to see the glory of God in Christ, and because of the light of Christ, to again see the gift of all things to be enjoyed with gratitude. It hurts, but I am thankful."

—Robert Campbell
Pastor of Santa Margarita Community Church
Author of *You are Here: Following Jesus, All the Way Down to the Dirt*

"Ronnie is a contrarian, an original thinker and a true catalyst. Every opportunity I get to be around him is a blessing to my soul. This book will enlighten, inspire and equip you."

—Michael Crawford
Pastor of Freedom Church
Maryland State Director of Missions (SBC)
Author of *100 Meditations: An Every Day Book for Every Day People*

"This book is on point; a tremendous help to anyone who has ever opened their mouth to speak! Ronnie gives great examples of how our complaining affects us—the shame it brings and how it humbles us—all while speaking deep truth with wisdom into the blind spot of complaining, leading us back to truth and hope to overcome and see God more clearly beyond our complaints."

—Amanda Edmondson
Co-Leader of Women's Ministry at Sojourn Community Church
Associate Editor of Gospeltaboo.com

"As a complainer, I need this book. Call it a hunch, but you need it too! Rich with stories and winsome in style, Ronnie invites us on his grouchy journey and pastors the reader down the path towards freedom. Who knew a book written by a complainer, and for complainers, about complaining could be so gratifying."

—Dave Harvey
Author of *When Sinners Say I Do* and *Am I Called?*
Pastor of Four Oaks Church
Executive Director of Sojourn Network

"Ronnie Martin has given us the book every leader has wanted to write but lacked the grace to do so well. With biblical clarity, theological insight and chuckle-producing wit, Martin speaks truth to our pride. Read the book and you'll fully understand the destructive nature of a complaining spirit and the wonderful ways you can replace it with gratitude. Seriously, read this book before someone gifts it to you anonymously."

—David Hegg
Pastor of Grace Baptist Church
Author of *The Obedience Option*

"As its title suggests, this book strikes at the heart of one of my biggest sin issues: complaining. With humor, candor and biblical truth, Ronnie pulls back the curtain on one of our favorite 'acceptable' sins and exposes it for what it is—a fundamental distrust in the goodness and sovereignty of a Lord who loves us and is ever working for our good and His glory. Read this book, be challenged by it, and replace your complaining with gratitude."

—Ted Kluck
Co-author of *Why We're Not Emergent* and *Household Gods*

"I didn't want to read this book because I knew that I needed to read it, but I'm glad I did. With both keen insight and dry wit, my friend Ronnie explores our all-too-common sinful tendency to grumble and offers grace-laced answers to our problem. You may not want to read *Stop Your Complaining* either, but you'll be glad you did."

—Matthew C. Mitchell
Pastor of Lanse Evangelical Free Church
Author of *Resisting Gossip*

"Ronnie Martin probes the heart in *Stop Your Complaining* and gives us an antidote to our faithless whining. By examining the biblical roots and vile fruits of complaining, Ronnie helps us escape the malaise of malcontentment. *Stop Your Complaining* is a needed rebuke and powerful recipe for grateful life with God and others."

—Daniel Montgomery
Lead Pastor of Sojourn Community Church, Louisville
Co-author of *Faithmapping* and *PROOF*

"I am adept at finding the downside in things. So reading Ronnie's book was a bit like jumping into a frigid lake. Martin reveals truth and digs into the reader without preaching or nagging or condescending. Instead he shares stories, his own and others. He asks questions and invites us to do the same. *Stop Your Complaining* is a book that would benefit anyone but the most ardent optimist."

—Barnabas Piper
Author of *The Pastor's Kid* and *Help My Unbelief*
Co-host of the *Happy Rant* (podcast)

STOP YOUR COMPLAINING

From Grumbling to Gratitude

Ronnie Martin

PUBLICATIONS
Fort Washington, PA 19034

Stop Your Complaining
Published by CLC Publications

U.S.A.
P.O. Box 1449, Fort Washington, PA 19034

UNITED KINGDOM
CLC International (UK)
Unit 5, Glendale Avenue, Sandycroft, Flintshire, CH5 2QP

Printed in the United States of America.

ISBN (trade paper): 978-1-61958-205-7
ISBN (e-book): 978-1-61958-206-4

Unless otherwise noted, Scripture quotations are from the Holy
Bible, ESV®, ©2001 by Crossway Bibles, a publishing ministry of
Good News Publishers. Used by permission.

Italics in Scripture quotations are the emphasis of the author.

DEDICATION

For all the whiners. We've been heard . . . long enough.

CONTENTS

FOREWORD

Growing up on a farm in South Dakota gave us a lot of opportunities for grumbling. Corn prices were never high enough. The weather was always too hot or too cold, too wet or too dry. Our neighbors took vacations we couldn't afford. Our relatives lived too close. Our politicians didn't have a clue. Our sports teams never won.

Since then I've lived in wealthier suburbs in the Midwest, Northeast, and South. But these people aren't much different from the farm folks of my youth. We still complain about the weather. We still complain about our neighbors. We still complain about the cost of things. We still complain about our government. We still complain about our coaches. It turns out grumbling unites people across geographic, ethnic and economic lines. The next time you meet a stranger, see how long it takes before you try to bond over common grievances.

Is this just a harmless form of human bonding? Or does it reveal something deeper, something more sinister, even an offense to the God who created the heavens and the earth? Can the grumbling heart also rejoice in the Lord?

In Philippians 4:4, the apostle Paul commands believers in Christ to rejoice. In case you missed it the first time, he immediately repeats the command. But rejoicing isn't something you can just force yourself to do. It doesn't come naturally to us the way grumbling does. We let our disagreeableness be known to everyone with every sarcastic quip about how we never get any breaks.

How does this attitude tell the world the Lord is at hand (see Phil. 4:5)? Because Christ has come for sinners, we can offer all our concerns, fears, worries and faint hopes to God in prayer with thanksgiving, so we need not be anxious about anything (see 4:6). Then the peace of God that surpasses all understanding will guard our hearts and minds in Christ Jesus (see 4:7). What would we rather have: the comfort of complaint or the character of Christ?

Imagine that when friends and family gathered around you they thought about whatever is true, honorable, just, pure, lovely, commendable, excellent and praiseworthy (see 4:8). Imagine that your words and actions showed the world that the God of peace is with you (see 4:9). But you can do more than imagine. This life belongs to you in Christ when you have repented of sin and trusted in his death and resurrection for you. If you know God, then "he who began a good work in you will bring it to completion at the day of Jesus Christ" (see 1:6).

My friend Ronnie Martin has written a convicting, challenging book that deserves wide reading in a world of plenty—of complaining. He writes as a pastor who hears a lot of grumbling, but he does not ignore this problem in his own life or even among fellow pastors. You might not initially think you should pick up a book about grumbling. You might have a friend or family member in mind who needs it more (good luck handing the book out as a birthday or Christmas gift). But I suspect you need the book more than you realize. I know I did.

Collin Hansen
Editorial Director for The Gospel Coalition and author of
*Blind Spots: Becoming a Courageous, Compassionate,
and Commissioned Church*

ACKNOWLEDGEMENTS

I'm not sure a book like this would have been written without the persevering and long-suffering heart of my wife, Melissa, who has been married to the chief of all grumblers for over twenty years. Thank you for being a true model of love, grace and gratefulness to me!

To my Substance Church family, including Dave Dernlan and Jeff Powell—It's a humble privilege to lead this church alongside both of you.

Many thanks to Andrew Wolgemuth, who has been a picture of encouragement and grace to me.

To the EFCA, Sojourn Network and the Gospel Coalition, my brothers and sisters in arms—thank you.

Thank you to David Almack, Scott Endicott, Erika Cobb and all at CLC Publications for taking a chance on a book that will, let's face it, not be incredibly enjoyable for someone to actually give to somebody else.

INTRODUCTION

It snows a lot in February.

It wasn't always this way. Not for me, anyway.

Up until five years ago, I lived in Southern California, which is far more sunny than it is snowy. As you might imagine, it's been an adjustment. In Southern California, things never really slow down. People are able to do all the things they want to do all year round because the weather never prevents them from doing so.

Ohio is different, of course. We have these things called seasons; these beautiful canopies of weather that descend upon us to create a rich and challenging diversity for us to live our lives under during the year. In this way, the seasons tend to mirror the lives God has given us, lives that include light and darkness, warmth and coldness, brightness and starkness.

As I write, the landscape is covered in a blanket of snow. Every couple of days it seems like another snowfall emerges, delaying spring yet another hour, another day. The trees are slender and bare. The temperature is frosty, usually below ten degrees. Some days, it feels claustrophobic and many of us start feeling isolated. There are times when some of us can't remember the last time we saw the sun. Some people can become despondent.

"I'm so tired of this snow."

"I hate the winter."

"It depresses me."

"I told my wife that I don't know if I can take another year of the cold."

It seems like I hear these same complaints every year. At which point I always think, it's not like we didn't know this was coming, right? It's not like Ohio used to be next to Texas and God decided to pack it up one year and relocate it to the Northeast. No, every year at approximately the same time, this white powdery stuff called snow falls from the heavens onto the ground of Ohio. Yet, all sarcasm aside, we complain about it just like the Israelites complained about the manna that came from heaven every morning to feed their families. We don't see snow as this beautiful thing that God created and lets fall in certain regions of the world where it gets cold enough to come down. Instead, we complain.

But a funny thing happens every year when March and April arrive. It stops snowing. The sun emerges. The temperatures start rising. And all around, the hills and trees turn the most vibrant, beautiful shades of green you've ever seen. But it didn't just happen. There's a reason why the colors are so deep and the landscape so rich. It's the snow. That's what we forget.

And isn't that the very definition of complaining? It's forgetfulness. It's forgetting who God is. That He's good, that He's jealous for His glory and that because of who He is, everything He does will always be for our good and His glory. This is a book to warn us about a not-often-talked-about sin that can have deep and dramatic consequences in the life of the Christian. It's a sin that stifles our communication with God, chips away at the joy of our salvation in Christ and tempts others to sin and doubt the grace of God who has graciously given us all things (see Rom. 8:32). Let us continue to remember this great grace as we seek to have hearts that overflow with gratefulness rather than grumbling.

PART 1

LOCATING COMPLAINING

1

THE ART OF COMPLAINING

"For although they knew God, they did not honor him as God or give thanks to him, but they became futile in their thinking, and their foolish hearts were darkened."

Romans 1:21

"YOU'RE going to write a book on complaining? I'd like to read THAT."

—Melissa Martin, a.k.a my wife

By way of introduction, let me be as straight as possible with you by admitting something that anyone who's known me for even a short amount of time would know: I'm a complainer. What I mean is, I grumble and whine about things that don't go my way. If you talk to my wife Melissa, she'll tell you I have a reputation (hopefully a diminishing one, by God's grace) for ranting and raving about things that annoy me and get easily under my skin. There have been countless moments when I roll my eyes widely and sigh loudly when situations don't pan out the way I want them to pan out, which seems to happen a lot, by the way. Depending on the day, I can be a glass-half-empty-not-super-fun-to-be-around kind of a guy. And believe me when I tell you that it wasn't super fun writing that last sentence.

Complaining is more than just a cute adjective to describe us on our bad days. In all of its various forms and functions it's become a lifestyle, a way of existence and a daily routine that is as natural to us as breathing, walking and eating. It's built into the foundation of our communication, bridging cultures together as one of the few ways we know how to relate to one another. Comedians build careers on it, car salesmen sell wheels with it, while the rest of us hone our skill at it like a veritable art form. It informs casual conversations with friends and intimate exchanges with loved ones. Complaining is not something we do, it's who we are on almost every micro and macro level imaginable. It's settled itself into the framework of our subconscious thoughts and saturates the sentences of our conscious talk. I'll go so far to say that without complaining, we'd probably lack the engine we have to drive the number of status updates on Facebook and Twitter into the stratosphere.

It can even be hereditary, in a sense.

I was born into a family of complainers. It was part of our dialogue, our humor and our way of relating to one another. When there was nothing to talk about and we were trying to avoid confrontation, complaining kept us from being too transparent and vulnerable, while still fooling us into thinking that we were actually sharing our hearts and pleading for a little empathy from the other person. My dad was known as the patriarch complainer of the Family Martin. Anytime something didn't go his way—the Dodgers lost the game, the Angels won the game, the food was cold, it rained after he washed his vehicle, he lost the Monopoly tournament, got stuck behind a slow driver or didn't get the good parking spot—he let the world, or in our case, the family, know that he was the one who always got the bad breaks. Interestingly enough, people who knew my dad well kind of loved this about him, and they sort of had to, because it was who he was.

One of the other inherent dangers of complaining is that we don't even realize we do it. It's become such a normal part of the directional flow and tonal shape of our conversations that nobody even notices.

And you know the worst part about it? Whether we realize we're doing it or not, we actually love it. It's addicting. It feeds upon itself, always wanting more and never getting enough. Complaining fuels an insatiable machine of moving parts inside our hearts that seeks to verbally capitalize on our endless state of discontentment.

Ever had a casual conversation that went something like this?

"Nice weather we're having, huh?"

"Yeah, it's beautiful."

"Well, it should be after the winter we had this year."

"No kidding."

"I'm sure there's a thunderstorm on the horizon to remind us it won't be this nice forever."

"Nothing lasts forever, that's for sure."

"This weather sure won't."

You see what happened there? A light conversation about the loveliness of the weather turned cynical and unlovely within seconds.

Here's another conversation I had at Best Buy as I made my way up to the counter to make a purchase.

"How's it going?" I asked the girl at the register while I fumbled for my wallet.

"Oh, you know, just living the dream," she replied, practically rolling her eyes at what was apparently a grossly insulting question.

Am I making a too big of a deal over a couple of seemingly irrelevant conversations? I'd say yes if these were simply a couple of rare, isolated exchanges that occasionally dropped into an ocean of fruitful discussions, but they're not.

What Is It Really?

"So what's the problem here?" you're thinking. "I get it, we're a nation of ingrates, a generation of grumblers, a massive collection of malcontents. Tell me something I don't know," you say. The problem, of course, is that this is a problem with deep roots that travel deep into the soil of our hearts. Complaining is sneaky and subtle, which is what makes it so poisonous for the Christian.

So if it truly is a slow poison in the spiritual veins of believers, how do we extract it and make sure it has no place in our lives? That is the heart of the question we want to ask, and for which we want to find biblical answers and practical solutions.

First things first though. Although complaining is subtle and may not sound serious enough to deserve an entire (though thankfully short) book written about it, the reality is that God calls complaining a sin. And all of our sins were serious enough for God to send His Son to die a costly death in order to pay for them all.

Looking back at the Old Testament, there were some serious repercussions for the children of Israel when they complained against the Lord.

In the book of Numbers, the Lord says to Moses, "How long will this people despise me? How long will they not believe in me in spite of all the signs I have done among them? I will strike them with the pestilence and disinherit them, and I will make of you a nation greater and mightier than they" (14:11–12).

Later in the chapter, the Lord again asks the question, "How long shall this wicked congregation grumble against me?" (14:27).

So before we go any further, we need to establish that, the Lord is not deaf or immune to the complaints of His people. When He heard the Israelites complaining to Moses about the lack of variety in their diet, for example, He rightfully took their dissatisfaction as not against Moses, but directly against Himself and His provision. Moses says in Exodus, "Your grumbling is not against us but against the LORD" (16:8). So although God is infinitely compassionate and sympathetic to our pleas for mercy, grace, justice and peace, He is equally displeased when our mouths communicate our own displeasure and disbelief in His goodness and grace.

With that said, let's talk. What is complaining, exactly? Is it really this big, gross sin or just one of these things we need to keep an eye on, like eating too much junk food, spending too much time on the computer, or anything in life that is ok to indulge in a little bit as long as we apply a bit of moderation to it?

A working definition for complaining is simply this: expressing dissatisfaction or annoyance about a state of affairs or an event.[1]

Let's take a minute to unpack the implications of this.

Complaining is an expression. It's expressing thoughts and ideas with our mouths that originated in our hearts before transferring to our minds. As someone who has spent twenty-five plus years working in the music industry, I've been constantly engaged in some form of what we call artistic expression, whether it's been from me or from other artists I've had the privilege of working with.

For example, I've known guitar players who move masterfully across the necks of their guitars, expressing excitement and energy through intricately played arpeggios and slides across the strings. I've recorded pianists who glide effortlessly across the ivories, playing notes and arrangements that evoke a refined, elegant and classical beauty. I've also worked with avant-garde and experimental artists who create stark and minimal musical passages, in an effort to express feelings of isolation and sadness.

What all of these artists have in common is that they're expressionists, and their instruments are simply the media they've chosen to communicate the thoughts and ideas that originated in their hearts.

Complaining is the expression of thoughts that find their origins in the depths of our hearts. It is a manifestation of our thoughts of dissatisfaction, annoyance, discontentment, bitterness, envy, anger, impatience and hate.

And our mouths are the instruments. Our speech has the power to settle into the hearts of others the very things that are springing out of our hearts. The book of James takes it far more seriously than most of us do, describing our tongues as being unrighteous, evil and untamable.

> And the tongue is a fire, a world of unrighteousness. The tongue is set among our members, staining the whole body, setting on fire the entire course of life, and set on fire by hell. For every kind of beast and bird, of reptile and sea creature, can be tamed and has been tamed by mankind, but no human being can tame the tongue. It is a restless evil, full of deadly poison. (3:6–8)

What is complaining if not a particular outflow of the untamed tongue? It is essentially our insistent refusal to be thankful for what we have and to show proper gratefulness by the fruit of our actions. What's concerning is that it rests side by side with the same affections we have for those things we express gratitude and praise for. James says that this type of verbal expression should not characterize the lives of those whose hearts have been made new again by Christ.

> With it we bless our Lord and Father, and with it we curse people who are made in the likeness of God. From the same mouth come blessing and cursing. My brothers, these things ought not to be so. Does a spring pour forth from the same opening both fresh and salt water? Can a fig tree, my brothers, bear olives, or a grapevine produce figs? Neither can a salt pond yield fresh water. (James 3:9-12)

James uses nature as a way of describing two opposing elements coming out of something that only has the ability to produce the one thing God has intended for it to produce. And yet, we live this out time and time again.

Think of how many times a perfectly good evening's been ruined when "out of the blue" something critical or unkind comes shooting out of our mouths. For the person on the receiving end, it can feel like it's coming out of nowhere. In reality, it's a heart condition and sin that's gone unchecked and hasn't been repented of, and when the "right" moment arrives it comes rushing out of you like lava from a volcano.

Sometimes it shocks the one it's coming out of, too! I remember a moment when Melissa and I were walking in the neighborhood and a person drove by who was part of a church we'd previously been a part of. He pulled up alongside of us and made a couple of harmless remarks that I reacted to by snapping at him in the worst way imaginable. He hadn't said anything wrong, but some of the anger and hurt I'd experienced had not been dealt with as thoroughly as I had thought.

He drove away and my wife stood there, practically speechless. How could I have reacted so aggressive and unkindly? It was like there was a hibernating bear inside me that suddenly woke up and realized he hadn't eaten for a while. Our heart forms the expression of our words, so what comes out is always dependent on what is already inside. What is lacking in the heart of a complainer is thankfulness, and a lack of thankfulness ultimately points to a lack of remembrance of God's goodness, greatness, sovereignty and staggering control over the intricate and intimate details of our existence.

That's where it ends up. But where does complaining begin? According to the Bible, it begins in our hearts. Jeremiah 17:9 tells us that "The heart is deceitful above all things, and desperately sick; who can understand it?"

What this means for us is that complaining is a symptom of something far more serious going on beneath the surface. According to the prophet Jeremiah, when we complain, we're expressing something that is coming from a sick and deceitful place, a place that can't be trusted to communicate what is true. It means that every time we open our mouths, words have the potential to reflect the very worst aspect of our fallen natures.

Complaining is a lack of self-control, choosing not to constrain our words because we're deceived in believing we're justified in voicing them. Like the time I embarrassingly lost my temper at a tire store because the mechanic claimed I needed four new tires instead of two, which is all I thought was necessary. In a matter of seconds I accused him of being a thief, yelled over the top of him, threw my hands in the air and stomped away in disgust. I apologized later, but I, along with my wife, was shocked at how badly I mishandled the moment. The mechanic was right, I did need four new tires, but my words reflected a heart that had deceived my mind and turned against another person. It's in these moments that our hearts replace hope with hatred, delight with disgust, encouragement with discouragement—and the list goes on.

Ultimately, complaining is the verbal communication of this very real lie: God got it wrong.

I Want To Do What I Want To Do

One of the most memorable scenes in Frank Capra's holiday classic *It's A Wonderful Life* sees the amiable George Bailey (played by the legendary Jimmy Stewart) visiting the home of potential sweetheart Mary Hatch (played by the equally iconic Donna Reed), who has just graduated college and returned to the small town comforts of her mother's home in Bedford Falls. After four years away, Mary finds George, her lifelong crush, an angry, disillusioned, frustrated young man. Every time it looked like George had the opportunity to leave Bedford Falls to pursue his dreams in the big city, something seemed to thwart him. So now he sits sulking in Mary's living room, complaining and irritable and in a sour mood.

Minutes later, Mary receives a phone call from their old high school pal Sam Wainwright, who offers George a deal to get in on the ground floor of a plastics factory he wants to open in Bedford Falls. The scene culminates with George grabbing Mary's arms as the phone plummets to the ground and in a rush of frustrated emotion he cries, "Now you listen to me, I don't want any plastics or any ground floors, and I don't want to get married ever to anyone, you understand that? I want to do what I want to do!"

Of course, George's rather abrupt handling of Mary turns into a passionate embrace, as he sees the love she has for him in her tear-filled eyes, causing him to realize he has always loved her, too. They're married in the very next scene.

I know, it's Hollywood.

Nevertheless, after a few years, we find that George hasn't really moved on from his struggles with bitterness and discontentment.

His marriage to Mary, along with the arrival of their four children, has not been enough to satisfy him. He still feels like a small man in a small town, and despises having to run the small Building and Loan he inherited from his father.

So what was wrong with George? After all, he really did have a wonderful life, as his guardian angel Clarence so aptly reveals to him by the end of the movie. So what was the issue?

As it is for many of us, the heart of George Bailey's dissatisfaction was believing the lie in his heart that the life he'd been given wasn't good enough and whoever gave it to him had gotten it all wrong. Because he never stopped believing that lie, he became an angry, fed up, complaining curmudgeon.

What happened to George could be traced back to the expectations he had created for himself as a boy. George had always dreamed of heading to the big city. It was a life pursuit that had turned into a life-consuming idol. All his plans had methodically unraveled one by one. His expectation of becoming a world-renowned architect had slowly slipped out of his grasp with every climactic turn of events until it was just a memory that fit somewhere between marriage and mortgage payments. But was George's life really that bad? No, most people thought it was great, but it simply wasn't how he imagined it. His ambitions had been placed in a theoretical life, until reality clashed with his fantasy.

The problem with George is the same problem most of us have, and it's that we believe that God is actively working against us, not giving us what's truly good for us. We express our disappointment and discontentment by complaining about it all.

But not everything has to be as monumental as the fictionalized life of George Bailey, does it? Don't we have the right to complain about some of the small things? Is that really so harm-ful? Because stuff happens, right?

My boss really does treat me badly, my car breaks down, my house needs repairs, my neighbor annoys me, my friend never calls me back, my spouse never affirms me, my kids drain me, my teacher is out to get me, etc.

Is it fair for me to get tagged as a "complainer" because I need to air some grievances and get some things off my chest? Isn't that better than keeping things pent up inside until I feel like I'm ready to explode?

Maybe, but what we'll see moving ahead is that complaining is not so much something we do, as something we are. In other words, because we were all conceived as sinners who don't nat-urally seek God, it's only natural for us to complain against God. Even after God's grace invades our dead hearts and turns our gaze back to Him, we will need that same grace to guard us against our fleshly tendency to grumble against God instead of being grateful to Him.

Whatever our reasoning may be, it's fair to say that most of us have mastered the art of complaining. Like gossip, complain-ing is a slow, subtle poison that builds in our systems and usu-ally goes undetected. It may be one of the least discussed sins in churches today. Nevertheless, we've seen from this chapter that it's a grievous sin against the Lord.

But let's get back to the question posed earlier. Is all com-plaining a sin?

If we define complaining as an expression of our dissatis-faction, the questions we have to ask are, what are we dissatis-fied with, why are we dissatisfied with it and finally, what does the Bible say about dissatisfaction? Is there really such a thing as what some call "holy discontentment" or is that simply a way for Christians to justify doing a little "holy complaining"?

Reflection Questions

1. Have you ever thought of yourself as a complainer?
2. What are some recurring complaints that you find yourself returning to often?
3. What are some of the deeper issues you can trace your complaints to?

2

HOLY COMPLAINING

*"Evening and morning and at noon I utter my complaint and moan,
and he hears my voice."*

Psalm 55:17

*"Guard your thoughts, and there will be little fear
about your actions."*

—J.C. Ryle

It had been three long years since I'd moved my family across the country for a new ministry position. To put it plainly, things were not working out. There had been troubling signs since the beginning, and later, conflicts everywhere. Arguments and strife had become the norm. A culture of distrust permeated the church staff I was now a part of, where unspoken and unresolved issues of bitterness and dysfunction appeared to have gone undealt with for years. My wife and I felt like we were in the throes of endless exhaustion and exasperation. The disappointment was overwhelming and the mounting fear of our future felt more and more paralyzing.

In the midst of it all, I was complaining incessantly. What was God doing? Did we really move over halfway across the country to fail so monumentally? Were we simply going to be another casualty in a long line of ministry missteps? Or was there another reason, another calling, another purpose for us in all the madness?

After much prayer, many tears and mountainous helpings of good counsel, we thought there was. But part of what we wrestled with was this idea of what many have called a "holy discontent." Meaning, God will many times provide a healthy dissatisfaction with our current environment in order to move us to our next one.

Although there are some definite fine lines between holy and unholy discontent, I believe we see holy examples of it all through the pages of Scripture. It was right for Jacob to be discontent with the way his uncle, Laban, had been unfairly treating him despite years of faithful service (see Gen. 31). It was right for Joseph to be discontent for being locked in prison for a crime he hadn't committed (see Gen. 40). It was right for the children of Israel to be discontent under the slave labor they experienced in the land of Egypt (see Exod. 2). It was right for King David to cry out to God for deliverance against the heavy hand of his enemies (see Ps. 13).

For all of these men, it was right for them to want something else, to be dissatisfied with their current predicaments and to bare their soul about it before the Lord and men. God doesn't waste times like these but uses them to develop patience, long-suffering and prayerful hearts so that bitterness doesn't ensnare us in its deadly claws.

What Are We Doing Here?

The prophet Elijah had been having what many of us would consider to be a red letter day (see 1 Kings 18:20–46). In the face of what many would call perilous odds, he had called for a sudden-death match between himself and four hundred and fifty false prophets to see once and for all who the real God of Israel was. Was it the God of Abraham, Isaac and Jacob, or was it the false god Baal? The challenge was simple: build an altar to your god and then call on him to answer your call by lighting the altar on fire. The god who answered with fire would be the true and living God that the people would then serve and worship.

It was a painfully grueling day. The false prophets kicked off the proceedings by calling on their god Baal, but the day passed with not so much as even a peep out of the guy. After a round or two of mocking and ridicule, Elijah called on the true God of Israel who promptly consumed the altar and everything around it.

Elijah should've been on top of the world. In dominating fashion, God had granted him victory over Baal and over the false prophets who were immediately detained and destroyed. In addition, he prayed for an end to the three-year drought Israel was experiencing and God answered by opening up the sky with thundershowers. By anyone's standards, this was a banner day at the office.

But things took a downturn. After Queen Jezebel found out that Elijah had killed her prophets, she declared Elijah a dead man. Running for his life, he ended up alone in the secluded safety of the wilderness. At this point, Elijah was spent. He was tired, hungry and discouraged; the joy of his victory from the day before had worn off. He was running for his life and really wished it would just end anyway.

> "It is enough; now, O LORD, take away my life, for I am no better than my fathers." And he lay down and slept under a broom tree. And behold, an angel touched him and said to him, "Arise and eat." And he looked, and behold, there was at his head a cake baked on hot stones and a jar of water. And he ate and drank and lay down again. And the angel of

the LORD came again a second time and touched him and said, "Arise and eat, for the journey is too great for you." And he arose and ate and drank, and went in the strength of that food forty days and forty nights to Horeb, the mount of God. (1 Kings 19:4–8)

It's here that we see a great example of the Lord caring for the needs of His servant. He knows what Elijah's been through. He knows that he's emotionally spent, physically tired and mentally exhausted. Many of us can understand Elijah's reaction, even if upon first glance it feels extreme. We all have those moments when we feel like no matter what we do, we can't break free from the pressures and stresses of life bearing down on us, as if the whole world is against us. In Elijah's case, it was true, and probably a bit more serious. And yet God is faithful to nourish, strengthen and equip him for the journey that lies ahead. God was faithful despite Elijah's dramatic request to end it all.

There he came to a cave and lodged in it. And behold, the word of the LORD came to him, and he said to him, "What are you doing here, Elijah?" He said, "I have been very jealous for the LORD, the God of hosts. For the people of Israel have forsaken your covenant, thrown down your altars, and killed your prophets with the sword, and I, even I only, am left, and they seek my life, to take it away." (1 Kings 19:9–10)

What Elijah said was partially true. He had been jealous for the Lord. It was the desire of his heart that the people of Israel would turn from worshiping idols and return to worshiping and serving the true and living God. The ultimate aim of his heart was true, but he had sunk into the despair of self-pity, which caused him to miss the real truth when he poured out his emotions to the Lord. God answers Elijah's complaint by reminding him of the trustworthiness He had shown him on Mt. Carmel.

And he said, "Go out and stand on the mount before the LORD." And behold, the LORD passed by, and a great and strong wind tore the mountains and broke in pieces the rocks before the LORD, but the LORD was not in the wind. And after the wind an earthquake, but the LORD was not in the earthquake. And after the earthquake a fire, but the LORD was not in the fire. And after the fire the sound of a low whisper. And when Elijah heard it, he wrapped his face in his cloak and went out and stood at the entrance of the cave. And behold, there came a voice to him and said, "What are you doing here, Elijah?"

He said, "I have been very jealous for the LORD, the God of hosts. For the people of Israel have forsaken your covenant, thrown down your altars, and killed your prophets with the sword, and I, even I only, am left, and they seek my life, to take it away."

And the LORD said to him, "Go, return on your way to the wilderness of Damascus. And when you arrive, you shall anoint Hazael to be king over Syria. And Jehu the son of Nimshi you shall anoint to be king over Israel, and Elisha the son of Shaphat of Abel-meholah you shall anoint to be prophet in your place. And the one who escapes from the sword of Hazael shall Jehu put to death, and the one who escapes from the sword of Jehu shall Elisha put to death. Yet I will leave seven thousand in Israel, all the knees that have not bowed to Baal, and every mouth that has not kissed him." (1 Kings 19:11–18)

What are we to make of Elijah's reaction here? There's no arguing that he was a dissatisfied and discontent man. He'd been faithful to everything God had commanded him to do and yet he felt that his work had been futile. Was he wrong? Yes and no! Although it's true that not everyone in Israel had turned their hearts back to God, there was a remnant who had remained faithful to Him.

Elijah had lost sight of whom he was serving. His jealousness for the God of Israel, though good, had allowed him to believe that Israel's response to God fell squarely on his shoulders. It didn't! God called Elijah to be obedient and to communicate the word of the Lord to the people of Israel, and nothing more. Only God could change the hearts of Israelites and judge them for continuing to rebel against Him by worshiping other gods. It was God who was in control of the fate of the nation, not Elijah.

The Satisfaction of Our Dissatisfaction

C.S. Lewis once remarked that the problem with humans is that we're satisfied far too easily with things that could never really satisfy us.

> It would seem that Our Lord finds our desires not too strong, but too weak. We are half-hearted creatures, fooling about with drink and sex and ambition when infinite joy is offered us, like an ignorant child who wants to go on making mud pies in a slum because he cannot imagine what is meant by the offer of a holiday at the sea. We are far too easily pleased.[1]

By Lewis' reasoning, dissatisfaction is experienced when desires are fulfilled by things that have a far too limited emotional, spiritual and physical capacity to actually sustain them.

What's deceiving about dissatisfaction is that there must be some elusory moment of satisfaction experienced before dissatisfaction can set in. In other words, to be become dissatisfied, one must first have a real or imagined satisfaction from which dissatisfaction can derive.

For example, a dating relationship usually begins with a high level of satisfaction, which typically includes an immediate attraction to the other person on a multitude of physical and emotional levels. You're inquisitive about their interests, concerned about their fears, curious about their past, interested in their hopes, curious about their dreams, thrilled by their appearance and admiring of their talents. The answers we receive from those initial inquiries help determine whether we believe a continued investment in that person is worthwhile.

However long or short-lived it is, there's a satisfaction that accompanies those early moments of realization.

The question is, are those things sustainable? Will those initial satisfactions be enough to carry you through the disillusionment that comes with time and familiarity? You could apply the same question to a number of other things.

For as long as he was alive, my dad would typically buy a new car every three years. About six months before he made his purchase, he would start dropping by dealerships, collecting brochures and narrowing his choices down to two or three models. Of course, the car he was driving while looking for his new car was the car he had been salivating over only two years before. At some point, the new car had become the old car. There were usually a couple of scratches and dents, the upholstery was stained, there was a ding in the window and the tires needed to be replaced. It had lost its luster. It was no longer the shiny prize he had driven off the showroom floor. It wasn't satisfying his desire for the ultimate driving experience.

Here's the thing: my dad wasn't under any illusion. Every time he bought a new car, he knew that it wouldn't take long before he wasn't satisfied with it any longer. Never once do I remember him telling me that he had found the ultimate vehicle and that this would be the last one he would ever buy. On the contrary, there was something in him that actually liked the satisfaction/ dissatisfaction roller coaster that led him to a new car purchase every three years. He knew that as soon as his satisfaction waned, he would be able to work up an appetite for whatever vehicle he craved next. It was an endless cycle that never allowed him to reach any level of lasting contentment.

Like Lewis remarked, Dad was far too easily pleased. He had chased a pleasure so easily within the grasp of his heart that it vanished as quickly as it had appeared. The result was a wave of discontent that was anticipated and trackable every three years of his life. Of course, the problem for Dad wasn't the standard wear and tear that all vehicles experience, but the wear and tear that came with the endless cycle of pursuing something that always had the same outcome.

In the book of Ecclesiastes, King Solomon grieves over the vanity of vanishing pursuits when he says, "a man to whom God gives wealth, possessions, and honor, so that he lacks nothing of all that he desires, yet God does not give him power to enjoy them, but a stranger enjoys them. This is vanity; it is a grievous evil" (6:2).

We see this in the classic Bill Murray movie *Groundhog Day*, where Murray plays a grumpy, bitter weatherman who wakes up every morning living the same day over and over again. It isn't until he starts pursuing the happiness of someone other than himself that he finally wakes up to a new day. Murray's dissatisfaction and discontentment is encapsulated in a devotion to pleasing himself and himself alone. His deepest desires have to change, and it isn't until he sacrifices his own comfort and aims to please the woman he has fallen in love with (played by Andie MacDowell) that change finally occurrs.

Jesus talks about the deep desires of the heart in the book of John when He says, "You did not choose me, but I chose you and appointed you that you should go and bear fruit and that your fruit should abide, so that whatever you ask the Father in my name, he may give it to you" (15:16).

Jesus is talking about our deepest desires becoming what God deeply desires, which is the fruit of obedience to Him. When we ask for more of that lasting fruit, God will always grant that request.

What usually gets forgotten when we fret about holy complaining is the "holy" part. The part where God uses less-than-ideal circumstances to humble our hearts so that we seek His face.

In his classic book *Holiness*, J.C. Ryle says, "Holiness is the habit of being of one mind with God, according as we find His mind described in Scripture. It is the habit of agreeing in God's judgment—hating what He hates—loving what He loves—and measuring everything in this world by the standard of His Word."[2]

How do we love what God loves and hate what God hates unless we experience both the joy and affliction that accompanies both? How will we ever grow in greater likeness to Christ without the shedding and discarding of those sins that keep our appearance more likened to the form and features of the world?

God is fashioning, shaping and transforming His church to be a holy people before Him. Is it possible for our complaining to help color in some of the edges of that holiness? It might be, if it causes us to see God as greater than the sum total of our complaints. It's easy for Christians to mumble the words "God is great" before meals and during worship at church, but do you believe that God is actually greater? In other words, is He sufficient enough to return to at the height of your occasionally holy complaints?

The psalmist writes, "Why are you cast down, O my soul, and why are you in turmoil within me? Hope in God; for I shall again praise him, my salvation and my God" (Ps. 42:5–6).

The question is not really whether we have a legitimate gripe against God, but whether we will hope in Him and praise Him once again, remembering that He is our salvation and the God who ordains all things in order that all things might glorify Him.

Reflection Questions

1. What category do you think the majority of your complaining fits under: holy or unholy?

2. Trace the root of your dissatisfaction. What is God revealing to you through it?

3. Do you find yourself loving what God loves and hating what He hates, more and more? How does complaining slow that process?

3

THE ORIGINS OF COMPLAINING

"What has been is what will be, and what has been done is what will be done, and there is nothing new under the sun."

Ecclesiastes 1:9

"As the salt flavors every drop in the Atlantic, so does sin affect every atom of our nature."

—Charles Spurgeon

Every summer, my dad would pack up the family and take us on our yearly family vacation. Most of the time, we'd spend it in the hot, hipster desert community of Palm Springs, California. Vacation for my dad consisted of renting a house with a pool and then spending a week or so doing nothing more than watching the family as we swam in 110-degree heat and devoured the vast array of goodies my mom would keep steadily supplied at the kitchen table. For a nine-year-old kid it was nothing short of glorious.

Then at night, we'd hop in our twelve-seat Ford Econoline van and hit the local steakhouse, where my dad would indulge in the delights of an expensive New York strip steak plus baked potato with all the trimmings. At some point after the meal, with a mile-wide look of gleeful satisfaction on his face, he'd lean back in his chair and exclaim, "Ahh . . . now this is living!"

And for Dad, it really was living. For one week in July, he was living his ideal. All the stresses and worries he carried concerning his business were left to be dealt with by his partner. His lifelong dream of owning a vacation home with a pool came temporarily true. The extravagance of eating out at expensive steakhouses every night (at least for a week) was finally attained. His vision of the ideal life was being realized, and for a brief period of time, he had no complaints.

But it didn't last long. Upon arriving home, Dad would plunge back into the daily grind of running a small business and supporting a family. The ideal had once again been swallowed up by the real. The glory of Eden was replaced by the grind of making ends meet: support a family, pay employees and satisfy customers.

Like my dad, we all have an ideal in our minds for the way life could or should be. For my dad, it was just getting to live a luxurious week free of worry about work and money, where leisure reigned supreme. So what's your ideal? Because whatever it is, it will be the expectation that you're constantly trying to live up to. And you will become disappointed when it's not being met. When the expectations of our minds aren't being met, we start to grumble. This is not a new thing.

Vintage Grumbling

All it takes is a trip to Genesis to see just how far back our complaining really goes. In the beginning, God created an ideal world, and everything He created He declared good because it was a perfect reflection of His glory and the design He had laid out for all of mankind. Then on the sixth day, after putting the universe and world in order, He created Adam and Eve, two people who would bear God's image, care for God's creation and be ideal companions for one another.

So in the beginning, we get a vision of God's ideal. Mankind living in harmony with the earth, with the animals, with each other and most importantly, with God. Until one day, the craftiest animal God created approaches Eve and introduces an idea to her that she has never considered before. The idea is a new one which causes her to question the ideal God had already given her.

> He said to the woman, "Did God actually say, 'You shall not eat of any tree in the garden'?" And the woman said to the serpent, "We may eat of the fruit of the trees in the garden, but God said, 'You shall not eat of the fruit of the tree that is in the midst of the garden, neither shall you touch it, lest you die.'" But the serpent said to the woman, "You will not surely die. For God knows that when you eat of it your eyes will be opened, and you will be like God, knowing good and evil." (Gen. 3:1–5)

A new voice had emerged in the garden. A voice that said something contradictory to the voice of the one who had formed and created Eve. A voice that told her that God had somehow gotten it wrong. Contrary to what God told her, the serpent informed her that she wouldn't die, but that the opposite would be true. Instead of death, she would actually become wiser, experience a fuller and more ideal life, the kind of life that God had been keeping her from.

So Eve believed the words of the serpent and ate the fruit that God had forbidden her to eat. And then she gave some to her husband Adam, who stood idly by, viewing what would be the most fateful dialogue in all of history. What happens next is not the stuff of legend but the everyday reality of men and women who must face the consequences of living in a fallen world. "Then the eyes of both were opened, and they knew that they were naked, and they sowed fig leaves together and made themselves loin cloths." (3:7).

Oddly enough, the serpent had been right. Their eyes were opened. But not opened to the infinite knowledge that only God could ever possess, but opened to their own nakedness, sin and shame. The hope they'd been promised of a new ideal came true, but what they didn't realize was that it would be so much less than the one they'd originally been promised.

And then this happened.

> [God] said, "Who told you that you were naked? Have you eaten of the tree of which I commanded you not eat?" The man said, "The woman whom you gave to be with me, she gave me the fruit of the tree, and I ate." Then the LORD God said to the woman, "What is this that you have done?" The woman said, "The serpent deceived me, and I ate." (Gen. 3:11–13)

There is a moment earlier in Genesis when we're told that a suitable helper couldn't be found for Adam. God had created the Garden of Eden for Adam to work in and cultivate, but it wasn't enough. God gave him control over the world's animal population to name and nurture, but it wasn't enough. There wasn't a suitable companion for Adam until God formed a new person from the person of Adam who could help fulfill and complete his physical, emotional and spiritual needs. Eve would be the ideal companion for Adam to sacrificially love, protect and serve, thereby modeling the love that God had shown him.

But Adam had failed. He hadn't loved, protected or served Eve the way that God had called him to. When the serpent approached Eve, Adam had just stood there, passively watching his wife be deceived by the world's greatest deceiver. Instead of rescuing Eve from the cataclysmic fate that God had graciously warned them about, Adam foolishly reacted to Eve's predicament by partaking of the fruit of death himself. Because of Adam's failure to guard his wife from deception, the entire world plunged into a downward spiral of deception, decay and death.

But it's the aftermath of this tragic state of affairs that I want to get to, because Adam's response to God's question is critical. It's accusatory in tone. It's blame-casting in content. It's . . . a complaint.

He says, "The woman whom you gave to be with me" (Gen. 3:12)—emphasis on the "you." What a different response to the one he had spoken earlier when he exclaimed, "This at last is bone of my bones and flesh of my flesh!" (2:23). The blessing of his wife Eve was now past tense for Adam. In his mind, she had gone from a helper to a hindrance, and his first inclination as a sinful human being was to blame God for the cause of it. But it wasn't true.

God's untarnished, unfading, idealized glory for Adam and Eve had been diminished by their choice. Everything had been traded for a lesser glory, and in reality, Adam's first response was one of dissatisfaction with his own choice.

A Lesser Glory

The seriousness of complaining lies at the root of what it really is, which is our natural dissatisfaction with a lesser glory. It wasn't that Eve could no longer satisfy Adam's need for a physical relationship. It was that Adam's greater need, a right relationship with God, had been severed. When that unraveled, Adam's relationship with Eve was never going to bridge the relational and spiritual hole that now existed in Adam's heart. His relationship with Eve would now appear far more pale, and he would now have a lifelong fight in his flesh to keep her from becoming an idol since the perfectly satisfying relationship he experienced with God had been broken.

What Adam and Eve inherited after being banished from the garden was a life lived among lesser glories. All the good creations of God they had once experienced in their ideal, perfected glory had now been corroded by sin, and would erode until death overtook them. Since perfection had been replaced with pollution, one of the most natural side effects to emerge would be the birth of complaining.

We get a small picture of this whenever we purchase something new. I remember when I got my first brand-new dirt bike. I had wanted it so badly until, finally, there it was, sitting in my garage, right off the showroom floor, perfect and untouched. I stood there for hours staring at it, talking about it, admiring it, sitting on it, visualizing the moment when I could finally get it in the dirt and ride it.

A day later, I wheeled the bike back to the garage after our first excursion at the racetrack, but it didn't look like the same machine I had started the day with. The plastic had some scratches on it, the decals on the tank were starting to peel off, and there were mud and dust in all kinds of hard-to-reach places. Feeling disappointed, I took the hose out, washed it down and did my best to return it to its original showroom condition, to no avail. It could never return to how it had been the day before. The elements had been too much for it. It would forever be a used bike from that moment on. Not surprisingly, I never loved it as much as I did on that first day before I'd ridden it, and I remember not being able to shake the horrible reality that it would never look as beautiful as it once did.

So I complained to my dad. I asked what we could do to keep my bike looking pristine. He suggested we cover up some of the scratches with decals and use some solvent to get rid of the more difficult stains. And yet, even at eleven years old, I knew this would only be a temporary fix. Unless every piece of the bike was replaced between every ride, or I simply never rode it again, I was going to have to accept the fact that my bike would be less than perfect until I bought something new again.

Our disappointment is not unfounded. It has roots. It comes from an innate longing and desire for things to remain new and beautiful. For things to retain their glory. Sadly, we know that nothing can, but it doesn't stop us from elevating lesser glories, hoping they might finally become the ultimate glories that we desire above all else. The result is always the same: we deceive ourselves, and that deception, like it did with Adam, leads to disappointment, ungratefulness and grumbling.

Complaining is casting blame on God. Adam was in effect saying, "This woman that *You* gave me caused my life to take a turn for the worse. It's not so much a decision I made as the decision You made that has now turned against me." Part of the deception of complaining is that it fools us into believing we're not responsible for our actions or for properly stewarding the lesser glories that God blesses us with.

Lesser glories are usually good things, by the way. They're things that God has created for our good that, when used in their proper context, can reflect the greater glory of the One who created and supplied them.

God has blessed me with a relationship with my wife that has its roots in what He established between Adam and Eve. There are intimacy, companionship and friendship that are glued together by love, mutual respect and a shared relationship with Christ. But it will always be less than my relationship with Christ. The minute I start expecting an ideal from my relationship with Melissa that can only be satisfied in Christ, what follows will be dissatisfaction, disappointment and grumbling.

The Rise of Corporate Complaining

With Adam's fall, death entered the world. "Therefore, just as sin came into the world through one man, and death through sin, and so death spread to all men because all sinned" (Rom. 5:12).

Each succeeding generation would suffer this cruel and unimaginable fate, because Adam's sin had infected the lifeblood of all who came after him. The fifth chapter of Genesis gives an account of the genealogies of Adam's descendants, each one ending with these three horrific words, "and he died."

But even this was a grace, considering that God had originally told Adam that in the day he ate of the forbidden fruit he would surely die. Instead of ending Adam and Eve's life the minute they sinned, He spared them. He gave them a long life and the ability to enjoy and cultivate their marriage relationship. He allowed them the blessing of having children. Death had entered the world yes, but it would be delayed by a long life in which one could choose to live obediently under God's commands.

But even before Adam, even before the foundations of the world, God decided to choose a group of people for Himself through whom He would end the cycle of death. It would be the single greatest act of love, grace and mercy in the history of mankind. Though it was Adam who rejected God's law and rebelled against Him, God would nevertheless redeem his cosmic ungratefulness with compassionate graciousness. So He raised up a man named Abraham, and a nation emerged from his grandson Jacob, who became a family of people known as the Israelites. They eventually became a mighty people, but before that happened, they were a large family who became slaves in a foreign land due to the consequences of some sinful choices made centuries earlier.

But after four hundred years of bondage under the mighty yoke of the Egyptians, they were finally being released. God had called a man named Moses to lead His people into the land He'd promised Abraham, Isaac and Jacob so many years before. The people had been suffering greatly under the heavy, oppressive hand of the Egyptians. The days were long, the work was back-breaking and the people cried out to God for deliverance.

But God heard the cries of His people and led them out of Egypt after a dramatic showdown between Moses and Pharaoh, the ruler of Egypt. God had kept His promises. He would deliver Israel from the Egyptians and bring them to a land He described as flowing with milk and honey. The journey would be difficult, but God would show His presence to the Israelites as a cloud during the day and a fire by night. After centuries of slavery, the Israelites were finally free. God had answered their cries for deliverance.

And then, almost immediately, the complaining began.

The people had barely pulled out of their driveways when the Egyptians came chasing after them. The Bible tells us that God had hardened Pharaoh's heart once again. He was aghast that he had just let the Israelites pick up and leave, so he decided to go round them up and bring them back to Egypt, like a parent retrieving a lost child. So the entire Egyptian army set out to bring the Israelite rebels home, and as soon as they came within eyeshot, the people quaked in their boots and cried out to Moses:

> "Is it because there are no graves in Egypt that you have taken us away to die in the wilderness? What have you done in bringing us out of Egypt? Is not this what we said to you in Egypt: 'Leave us alone that we may serve the Egyptians?'

For it would've been better for us to serve the Egyptians than to die in the wilderness." (Exod. 14:11–12)

The Lord had been faithful. He had heard their cries to be a free people once again. He had chosen Moses, a leader He had raised up and appointed from their own people. He had performed unbelievable signs and wonders in plain view of both nations. He had ravaged the land of Egypt while keeping the land the Israelites inhabited safe and untouched. He had spared them the death of their firstborn children while taking the lives of all the firstborn of Egypt. When Pharaoh finally released them, the Egyptian people sent them away with all manner of money, jewels and riches. The Lord had not simply bought the children of Israel a one-way ticket, He had equipped and prepared them well for their journey. He was the God of their fathers. He could be trusted. He could be relied upon to do what He said He would do. But like it does for many of us, a fear of man prevailed over a fear of God—over an acknowledgement that God had not abandoned them but would remain faithful to them.

Sadly, even after God allowed the Israelites to safely cross the Red Sea and then destroy the Egyptian army behind them, a pattern of grumbling and complaining had been established that would characterize an entire generation. When they were thirsty, they grumbled. When they were hungry, they grumbled. When they were tired of God's provisions, they grumbled. Like most of us, they had selective memories, constantly returning in their minds to the "glory days" in Egypt, forgetting the cruelty and mistreatment they and their children had been subjected to. Fear had kept them in Egypt all those years, and now fear had tricked them into pining away for a past that had been anything but glorious.

Primitive Fear

One of the primitive emotions you see at the heart of all grumbling and complaining is fear, which is expectation of, or worry about, something bad or unpleasant.

However great or small, there are expectations that lie at the heart of our grumbling. Whenever something experiences breakage in our lives, it causes us to fear it happening again. We complain because there's something happened before that we're afraid might happen again.

Ever catch an episode of *Winnie the Pooh*? All the characters in the Hundred Acre Wood have their personalities and quirks, but only one is known for being perpetually whiny and downcast all the time, and that's Eeyore. Whatever is happening, Eeyore can only see the potential downside of every situation. He's afraid to hope, lest his expectations be dashed to the ground and he won't be able to live with the letdown. For him, it's better not to hope at all and to just anticipate all the bad things that might happen so that he's not surprised when they do, which in his worldview is inevitable.

How many of us are like Eeyore? Fleshing out our fears in the form of complaining, instead of growing in godly hope, which "does not put us to shame, because God's love has been poured into our hearts through the Holy Spirit who has been given to us" (Rom. 5:5). What complaining displays in us is a lack of belief that God is who God says He is and that His love for us is not false, but true.

Paul says in Romans 5:1–5,

> Therefore, since we have been justified by faith, we have peace with God through our Lord Jesus Christ. Through him we have also obtained access by faith into this grace in which we stand, and we rejoice in hope of the glory of God. Not

only that, but we rejoice in our sufferings, knowing that suffering produces endurance, and endurance produces character, and character produces hope, and hope does not put us to shame, because God's love has been poured into our hearts through the Holy Spirit who has been given to us.

Justification by faith in Christ leads to peace with God that causes rejoicing even in suffering; a hope and endurance exist in us that are built upon a foundation of God's love, which we experience through the Holy Spirit. When this is believed, applied and meditated on, there will be no complaining.

Can you trace the origins of your complaining? Was there something in your past that causes you to grumble about the present so as to not be crushed by unrealized expectations for the future? Can you relate to the children of Israel? You've seen so many evidences of God working in your life, but you continuously fall back into the clutches of fear and doubt. Do you feel like a human version of Eeyore? Do you always snap back to a default mode of grumbling and complaining like there's a giant rubber band around your waist? Are you someone who, even when things are "going good," vocalizes reasons why they probably won't stay that way? Has complaining become a protection from the vulnerability that comes from being let down so many times?

In answer to those questions, take a hard look at some of the old and sinful layers in your life that have been obscuring your ability to rejoice in everything God has done and continues to do for you.

Eustace and the Dragon

C.S. Lewis opens up his third book in The Chronicles of Narnia, *The Voyage of the Dawn Treader*, by introducing a boy named Eustace Clarence Scrubb. A spoiled, disagreeable and whiny kid, Eustace is forced to spend a summer with his cousins, Edmund and Lucy Pevensie, whom he dislikes very much. As is the case with most of the Narnia books, the lion king Aslan eventually calls the characters to the land of Narnia to embark on a critical assignment in service to himself and his land. For Eustace, Edmund and Lucy, it means joining a voyage on a ship called the *Dawn Treader* to find some old explorers who had disappeared years earlier in their quest to reach the end of the world. For most of us, this sounds like the type of adventure that childhood dreams are made of, but not for Eustace. He's a miserable wreck from the minute the magic takes them on board the ship.

He whines, complains and sulks incessantly, oblivious to the magic and beauty that surrounds him as they take this spectacular and fantastic journey. Eustace remains unchanged until they arrive on a remote island, and he gets lost in a cave of gold that formerly belonged to a dragon. It's in this cave that that Eustace actually transforms into a dragon himself, finally becoming on the outside what he already was on the inside. It's this transformation that allows him to see the depth of his depravity and sin and feel remorse for who he was. It's not until Aslan comes to him and claws off the layers of dragon skin that Eustace can go back to being a boy again, albeit a reformed and changed one.

The process for Eustace was painful, but he'd been conditioned since he was a child to feel entitled to have whatever material comforts he thought he deserved. It didn't matter what anyone else thought, either. His god was comfort and he worshiped at its altar, fearful of when it might stop and incessantly complaining when it finally did.

The Sanctification of Discomfort

God does a gracious thing when He takes us out of our own "Egypts" and causes us to be in uncomfortable, unfamiliar, wilderness surroundings. He does a kind thing when He disciplines us like Eustace by revealing our idols through the absence of comfort and familiarity, when He doesn't leave us alone, but peels away the layers of self-worship that we inherited from our first parents. He does a gracious thing when He pulls us from the petty self-indulgence of our complaining and reminds us of the limitless awe and grandeur of Himself and His plan to redeem and restore all things through the miracle of Christ on the cross.

Regardless of what kind of past we can lay claim to, God is always pulling us toward the more comforting but not always comfortable hope of the gospel. It is the gospel that puts a horrific mirror in front of us to show the ugly disfigurement of our sin. The gospel shows us Christ being beaten and humiliated to the point of death before hanging and dying horrifically on a cross alongside murderers and thieves.

The gospel shows us our origins in Adam before giving us a future in the new Adam. The apostle Paul tells us in his first letter to the Corinthians, "For as by a man came death, by a man has come also the resurrection of the dead. For as in Adam all die, so also in Christ shall all be made alive" (15:21–22).

In Christ, our origins don't hold us in their grasp any longer. We are living in a new reality within a new community that doesn't have to fall headfirst into the cauldron of complaining any longer. "Therefore, if anyone is in Christ, he is a new creation. The old has passed away; behold, the new has come" (2 Cor. 5:17).

It's our identity as new creatures that enables us to respond to Christ with a new heart and new voice. Yet despite this new and glorious identity, our flesh is constantly fighting to show its old face again—a face that looks familiar and feels comfortable.

Reflection Questions

1. What are some of the lesser glories in your life you continue to pursue?
2. Name some of the layers that have built up that God needs to peel back.
3. What's something that's become increasingly uncomfortable to you? Do you need to repent of it?

4

THE COMFORT OF COMPLAINING

"How then will you comfort me with empty nothings?
There is nothing left of your answers but falsehood."

Job 21:34

"Whatever your heart clings to and confides in, that is really your
God, your functional savior."

—Martin Luther

Complaining feels good. As an expert in the field of Grade-A Grumbling, I can tell you that it's provided me with countless hours of intoxicatingly toxic conversations and mind-numbing meditative musings over the course of my lifetime.

I'd like to think that it's lessened somewhat since entering pastoral ministry, but there have been plenty of seasons in my life that would indicate it hasn't much. Since I spend quite a bit of time with ministry leaders, one of the temptations that constantly faces me is the camaraderie that comes from exchanging ministry struggles. Of course, it's a good and necessary thing to be able to share your heart with a fellow brother and pastor who is fighting the good fight right alongside you. Being able to listen, give wise counsel and receive that same encouragement is invaluable for these types of relationships to thrive. There can be a subtle downside, though, especially when you realize your interactions have become nothing more than cold, repetitive and comfortable marathon sessions of unending complaining. My problem (and sin) has been at the level in which I enjoy and feed off of it.

Of course, you don't have to be a pastor to become addicted to complaining, although this vocation might give you greater opportunity. Whether we like to admit it or not, there's something eerily satisfying about airing our ungrateful grievances to anyone who'll lend us an ear. Complaining can feel cathartic, like unloading a weighty burden off our shoulders. Other times it can feel like we're getting revenge against undeserved misfortune by exclaiming to the world that we've not gotten our just due.

Grumbling can also feel empowering. When people or circumstances make us feel powerless, we often seek personal justice through verbal self-victimization. It's not just verbal, either. Those conversations we have playing nonstop in our minds can be a running commentary of nonverbalized complaints and discontentment.

The bottom line is that if grumbling didn't feel so great, we probably wouldn't make a near profession out of it the way we do. It would be in a category with things like sticking fingers in electrical sockets or diving naked into freezing cold bodies of water at the height of winter. Actually, some people devoutly do that last one. The point is that there is some addictive level of satisfaction that comes from engaging in copious amounts of complaining that keeps us coming back for further feeding at its trough.

It had been one of "those days." Nonstop, chaotic and unsettling, where the hours feel long, the tasks are never done and there's an unspoken feeling of futility in the air. The problem was how many of this type of days my wife and I seemed to be having.

I think it's worth mentioning that we were under no illusions. When we planted Substance Church a couple of years back, we had what I think was a fairly accurate picture of the challenges that would face us. Most of our friends were other, more experienced church planters. So we saw the struggles firsthand and were able to acquire a good, clear view of some of the hard, thankless work that was characteristic of the "job." We were prepared to be tired, to have down days, to be uncertain of our future and to see how God might grow us regardless of whether He decided to grow "our church" or not. The one thing (maybe the only thing) we were certain of was that our small university town desperately needed a fresh, new gospel-centered church.

Miraculously, the Lord blessed our efforts. It didn't take long for a core group to emerge and before we knew it, we had a permanent meeting space in the heart of downtown, which was exactly the spot I had envisioned before planting. God definitely appeared to be blessing, but He also seemed to be doing it in double time. What we hadn't anticipated or even dreamed of was the speed at which He started growing us. In only a matter of months, God grew us from a twenty person core team to something five times that size. I know, we're not talking megachurch numbers here, but our impression was that we'd have plenty of time to slowly figure out all that we didn't have any clue about, which was basically . . . everything.

For those of you reading who don't know much about church planting, let me just say that it's a relentless undertaking. There's never a moment when something can't be worked on and something doesn't need to be done. There are people to pastor, sermons to prepare, documents to write, websites to maintain, a building to keep clean, chairs to set up, tables to tear down, food to be purchased, music to be rehearsed, community groups to be led, men's groups to be taught, elder meetings to attend, and those are just the day to day things that happen within a one-mile radius of where you live and worship. The point is, it's nonstop, because at this point in the life of the church you don't typically have a staff, you're still trying to build leaders and you're still throwing things at walls to see what will stick. In a word, it can be chaos, and sometimes the chaos comes to a crescendo. I remember one of the nights that it did.

There I was on Saturday night, pacing the floors, ranting and raving to my wife about everything under the sun, seeing the overwhelmed and despondent look on her face, knowing that in spite of the melodrama, most of what I was saying was true. And she would know, better than anyone. As much as I'd like to say that this was just a rare occurrence that sometimes happened at the end of a trying day, I really can't. My grumbling was very near the surface of my heart and ready to fly from my mouth with little prompting. Like all complaining, there was an odd sort of physical comfort to it, like somebody blowing off steam in the gym at the end of a stressful day. It reinforced my own pride and self-justification, with the allure of false assurance telling me that nothing was my issue. The truth I would come to learn was that the only issues we ever face are the ones inside our own hearts.

The Lord did something in that moment. My morning reading through Psalm 9 came faintly back into my mind. I stopped, looked into Melissa's beautiful, tired eyes and said, "Let's sit down."

She probably thought I wanted to transfer my hysteria to a more comfortable seating position, but I told her I wanted to do what David did in the psalm. So we looked each other in the eyes and gave thanks to God. And then we recounted all of the amazing deeds He had accomplished in our lives since planting Substance Church. We thanked Him for His faithful provision, for the people He kept bringing through the doors every week, for the men and women who were being discipled in our community groups and for the kindheartedness shown over and over again to us by "our people."

Before we knew it, we were shaking our heads at the foolishness that so easily descends upon us. My heart rate hadn't settled down, but it was "up" for the right reasons. We had reminded each other of the wonder of God's boundless provision. A God who was not just sovereign, but also infinitely kind, undeniably caring, unfailingly gracious and incredibly rich in mercy. We knew we didn't deserve a road any easier than the much harder roads traveled by countless faithful men and women before us. But we had to stop on the road we were going down and remember who it is that casts beams of great light onto our paths.

Jonah

One of the most interesting and instructive stories in the Bible is about an Old Testament prophet by the name of Jonah. If you've grown up in Sunday school, the name will immediately call to mind the whimsical tale of a whale who gobbles up a man running away from God. All of that is true, but there is so much more.

The story begins when God calls Jonah to do an overseas job assignment in a massive city called Nineveh. The wicked, unrighteous acts of the Ninevites had reached a point where God would not tolerate their evil deeds any longer, and He decides to cast judgment on them for it. Jonah's job is to travel to Nineveh and inform them that in forty days, God is going to destroy the city. Not an incredibly complicated task, but Jonah hates the assignment, because Nineveh is an enemy nation to the Israelites and Jonah knows there is a good chance that God might show them mercy and spare them if he starts preaching God's wrath against them.

So Jonah packs his bags, goes to the harbor and boards a cargo ship heading in the opposite direction! God isn't incredibly amused, so He causes a storm to break out against the ship. It's so severe that the crew's only idea for why it could possibly be happening is that someone must have angered their god. Jonah confirms their suspicions and has them throw him overboard. Miraculously, the waters calm down and the ship and entire crew are saved. Ironically, Jonah is saved too. Rather than letting him drown out in the middle of the sea, God sends a monstrous sea creature to swallow him up.

Three days later we find Jonah still alive in the belly of the fish, crying out miserably to the Lord for forgiveness. God hears Jonah's prayer and has the sea creature, who I'm guessing probably regretted this meal for the rest of his life, regurgitate him onto dry land. God hasn't forgotten about the task He'd originally assigned to Jonah, so He sends him there again to complete it.

This time Jonah obeys and marches from one end of Nineveh to the other, preaching the message that God told him to preach. Amazingly, the people listen! They take God's message to heart and repent! And God hears them and withholds His judgment! Then right on cue, Jonah throws a whopper of a temper tantrum.

> But it displeased Jonah exceedingly, and he was angry. And he prayed to the Lord and said, "O Lord, is not this what

I said when I was yet in my country? That is why I made haste to flee to Tarshish; for I knew that you are a gracious God and merciful, slow to anger and abounding in steadfast love, and relenting from disaster. Therefore now, O LORD, please take my life from me, for it is better for me to die than to live." And the LORD said, "Do you do well to be angry?" (Jon. 4:1–4)

So if you're like me, a couple of things immediately come to mind after reading Jonah's initial reaction to the mercy and grace God showed the Ninevites.

First off, our boy Jonah sounds a bit on the melodramatic side, doesn't he? He prays one of the oddest prayers recorded in the pages of Scripture, saying that because he knew he could count on God to be the gracious, merciful, patient and loving God that God is, it would be better for him to die than to see a nation he so hates and despises actually escape God's wrath. It didn't matter that Jonah was God's chosen prophet and spokesman for Israel. His heart had become so hard, calloused and bitter that he would rather die than see God allow people to live whom he believed should be destroyed.

Second is the fact that Jonah was arguing with God. His grumbling against the goodness of God made him forget who he was speaking to! His reverence and awe for the Lord were crushed beneath the layers of hate and prejudice he had let build and compound in his heart and mind. Although he acknowledged God's grace, mercy, patience and love, he didn't apply any of it to his own life. Jonah believed that God was misplacing His affections on a group of people who didn't deserve them, and it angered him to the point that he lost his desire to live.

It doesn't end there.

Jonah went out of the city and sat to the east of the city and made a booth for himself there. He sat under it in the shade, till he should see what would become of the city. Now the LORD God appointed a plant and made it come up over Jonah, that it might be a shade over his head, to save him from his discomfort. So Jonah was exceedingly glad because of the plant. But when dawn came up the next day, God appointed a worm that attacked the plant, so that it withered. When the sun rose, God appointed a scorching east wind, and the sun beat down on the head of Jonah so that he was faint. And he asked that he might die and said, "It is better for me to die than to live." (Jon. 4:5–8)

So after his initial rant, Jonah ignores God's question about the validity of his anger and stomps out of town hoping that God will still inflict His wrath on the people rather than receive their repentance. Jonah expresses what many of us would express in that moment, which is that these people deserve judgment. God is making a bad decision!

But God decides to show grace not only to the Ninevites, but also to Jonah by growing a plant over his head to shade him against the sun and wind. As Jonah relaxes under the plant, with a front row seat for what he hopes will be the annihilation of Nineveh, God appoints a hungry worm to gobble up his shady umbrella. First a whale and now a worm—we see how God uses both the big and the small to remove the idol of comfort from His saints. Oblivious to it all and ever the drama king, Jonah throws yet another hissy fit and once again exclaims that dying would be better than baking in the discomfort of the hot sun and scorching wind.

But God said to Jonah, "Do you do well to be angry for the plant?" And he said, "Yes, I do well to be angry, angry enough to die." And the LORD said, "You pity the plant, for which you did not labor, nor did you make it grow, which came into being in a night and perished in a night. And should not I pity Nineveh, that great city, in which there are more than 120,000 persons who do not know their right hand from their left, and also much cattle?" (4:9–11)

God poses the same question He asked Jonah the day before, "Do you do well to be angry?" Jonah doesn't waste any time on this one and emphatically replies, "Yes, angry enough to die!" As Jonah's discomfort in his surroundings intensifies, the comfort he found in complaining only increases. Jonah loses all sense of reason and reasonableness. His affections only go inward, and when those affections aren't being satisfied, his only response is to grumble in despair and disgust. Jonah can't find any comfort in the power of God's reconciling nature, because the supreme ruler in his life is his own unrepentant nature.

God very calmly reasons with Jonah and shows how hard and insensitive his heart has become. How he's gotten to the place where he cares more about the loss of a plant than about the loss of 120,000 people. Jonah had forgotten. He forgot that he himself had been spared from God's wrath after his own disobedience. He forgot that God had miraculously saved him from a dark, horrendous death at the bottom of the sea. He had forgotten because an ungrateful heart is a forgetful heart. And the expression of an ungrateful and forgetful heart is grumbling and complaining.

After you stop shaking your head in disbelief over the outrageous response of Jonah, think about your own. About how often you forget. Tally a list in your head of some of the ways God has been gracious and merciful to you and how, like Jonah, you've stormed off in forgetful oblivion because an immediate need was not being met in the way you wanted it to be. Think about how God has responded during those times when you've been far more grumbling than grateful for His provision. Did He cut you off? Lose His temper? No, He continued to show you grace upon grace! He showed you undeserved mercy.

Why Does It Feel So Good?

Satisfaction is not guaranteed. It never has been. If it was, the economy would sink into a quagmire, with consumers being replaced by a more conscientious culture who only sought after things they absolutely needed. Of course, this is the stuff of utopian sci-fi novels and op-ed columns in *Scientific American* magazine. The fact is that dissatisfaction runs rampant. We are rarely happy with what we have and hardly grateful for what we've been given. There's a vein that runs inside of us all that tells us things aren't good enough.

Complaining is an internal deception that gives way to a verbal reality. It's believing that we are entitled to something better than what we've been given. It's saying on one hand that we believe God is not really in control, but then being dissatisfied with His choices when we believe He is. It lacks logic. And it's addicting.

> But each person is tempted when he is lured and enticed by his own desire. Then desire when it has conceived gives birth to sin, and sin when it is fully grown brings forth death. (James 1:14–15)

The temptation to complain comes from a desire for something we don't have, and it's the lack of fulfillment of that desire that causes us to commit the sin of complaining. Unfortunately, it's a sin that is every bit as serious as all other sins, because sin taken to its logical conclusion ends in death.

James goes on to say this:

> Do not be deceived, my beloved brothers. Every good gift and every perfect gift is from above, coming down from the

> Father of lights with whom there is no variation or shadow
> due to change. (1:16–17)

James is reminding us that the good things we have are given to us by the good God who gives them, and He makes no mistakes in the giving.

Complaining becomes comfortable because it's padding over something far more insidious in our lives that we're not getting to the root of: ungratefulness.

In the book of Colossians, Paul instructs the church to "let the peace of Christ rule in your hearts, to which indeed you were called in one body. And be thankful. Let the word of Christ dwell in you richly, teaching and admonishing one another in all wisdom, singing psalms and hymns and spiritual songs, with thankfulness in your hearts to God" (3:15–16).

The only way to truly combat the comfort we get from complaining is for God's Word to take up total residence in our hearts and minds before anything comes out of our mouths. We must remember what God has done and repeat it often. David the psalmist writes, "I will give thanks to the Lord with my whole heart; I will recount all of your wonderful deeds" (Ps. 9:1).

If you've ever read anything about the life of David, you might conclude that he had some things to complain about over the course of his lifetime. Two of the main ones were the times when King Saul and when David's son Absalom were seeking to murder him. What David illustrates to us through many of his psalms is the heart of a man who didn't deny the troubling times he often found himself in, but who also didn't delight in victimization or allow it to mark the tone of his words. But don't a lot of the psalms sound like complaining, you ask? Only in the sense that they struggle to grasp God's sovereign purpose and wonder why He is doing the things that He's doing. What allowed David not to sink into the swamp of complaining is that he *gave thanks and recounted*.

David intentionally gave thanks to the Lord and recounted all the ways that God had been faithful to him through the years of his life. How easily he could've let his heart sink into bitterness and entitlement, but he guarded against it by turning back to the glory of who God is, and the unfailing surety of His mighty acts and wonderful deeds.

Why Is It So Hard to Stop?

In a strange way, grumbling is akin to being drunk. It's attempting to make something that feels bad on the inside feel "good" on the outside. Proverbs says "Who has woe? Who has sorrow? Who has strife? Who has complaining? Who has wounds without cause? Who has redness of eyes? Those who tarry long over wine; those who go to try mixed wine" (23:29–30).

Complaining is really just an accompaniment. It's the outflow of something far more critical stirring in our hearts. Like any drug, it's hard to stop because it's a numbing agent. If we were to communicate what's really going on inside, we would be exposing an uncomfortable and horrifying level of fear and distrust that would make us vulnerable to the truth. We complain to conceal truth, because truth is sometimes too unbearable to lay bare. What's much easier is settling on the feelings and emotions of a situation to hide our deeper fears.

John writes in his first epistle, "There is no fear in love, but perfect love casts out fear. For fear has to do with punishment, and whoever fears has not been perfected in love" (4:18). What does John mean by being "perfected in love"? He means the love of Christ, as displayed through the gospel, progressively transforming us more into the character of God. As this is happening, our grumbling will become less desirable and be replaced by a much greater desire for God's grace to be what shapes the thoughts that form the words coming out of our mouths. It means our preferences are being fought for and sanctified. John Piper says, "Preferring anything above Christ is the very essence of sin. It must be fought."[1]

It's hard to fight against something you love. And I love sitting down with a friend and family member with a story of some grievance that I know will cause a reaction and buy some morsel of sympathy. There's something inherent in me that feeds off this type of low-level but alluring satisfaction. I want someone to know that I didn't get what I deserved and I want them to affirm that yes, it's true: I did not get what I deserved! And then I want to hear a version of the same story from them so that I know I'm not alone and that bad things happen to other, equally as deserving people as me.

Come on, you say, is some casual complaining now and then really preferring something above Christ? Is it really the thing that's going to unwind my walk with Jesus? Does this really come from a sinful desire? James says it does: "Then desire when it has conceived gives birth to sin, and sin when it is fully grown brings forth death" (1:15).

Although a bit of casual whining and complaining can seem like a harmless exercise, it can become the cause for hard-heartedness before Christ. It speaks against the kind of speech that is most pleasing to God, which are words that "stir up one another to love and good works" (Heb. 10:24).

Paul talks about this in the book of Ephesians when he says,

> Look carefully then how you walk, not as unwise but as wise, making the best use of the time, because the days are

evil. Therefore do not be foolish, but understand what the will of the Lord is. And do not get drunk with wine, for that is debauchery, but be filled with the Spirit, addressing one another in psalms and hymns and spiritual songs, singing and making melody to the Lord with your heart, giving thanks always and for everything to God the Father in the name of our Lord Jesus Christ, submitting to one another out of reverence for Christ. (5:15–21)

Paul is saying to let the Holy Spirit shape the things that come out of your mouth to resemble the fruit He's producing in your heart. Speak to one another in song, let there be a tunefulness in your heart toward God, give unceasing thanks to Him for all He's done and sacrificially give yourself to one another. Complaining will seem increasingly ugly when you let the beauty of God's Word transform the words of your mouth.

Paul says to the Philippians, "for it is God who works in you, both to will and to work for his good pleasure. Do all things without grumbling or disputing, that you may be blameless and innocent, children of God without blemish in the midst of a crooked and twisted generation, among whom you shine as lights in the world" (Phil. 2:13–15).

The Christian can have utmost confidence that the work God is doing in His children is for His good pleasure. That's *good* pleasure, by the way. It's a goodness that we will reflect as we blamelessly and innocently represent our gracious God as shining lights among a crooked generation in a weary world. A world where we used to be blind to God's grace but can now rejoice in His vision to restore all things to Himself.

Blessed be the God and Father of our Lord Jesus Christ, the Father of mercies and God of all comfort, who comforts us in all our affliction, so that we may be able to comfort those who are in any affliction, with the comfort with which we ourselves are comforted by God. (2 Cor. 1:3–4)

For the last half of the book, we'll look into how God's grace accomplishes this in us.

Reflection Questions

1. Has complaining become a comfortable mode of communication in some of your relationships? Try connecting with a friend to discuss if this has become characteristic of your friendship.

2. What do we learn about God's character from the complaining of Jonah? How does He respond to Jonah's complaining?

3. Is there something in your life that complaining is concealing that's too painful for you to bear? Pray and meditate on Second Corinthians 1:3–4.

PART 2

COMBATING COMPLAINING

5

THE EXHAUSTING PURSUIT OF HAPPINESS AND THE INEXHAUSTIBLE WORK OF JOY

"These things I have spoken to you, that my joy may be in you, and that your joy may be full."

John 15:11

The pursuit of joy in God is not optional.

—John Piper

Do you remember happiness? That almost indefinable word that you grew up believing was the most important thing you could ever hope to attain? So how would you define it? As a feeling? An emotion? A lifestyle? A worldview? What the heck is it? It must be great since everyone's chasing after it; it also must be fairly elusive since everyone keeps chasing after it.

In this way, happiness is like a branch from an apple tree that's just out of reach, until that moment when it finally hangs low enough for us to reach out and pluck that golden piece of fruit.

One of the definitions of happiness is a "pleasurable or satisfying experience."[1] Most of us have had a few of those. It can be something small, like a bite-sized portion from a delicious entrée, or something big like a wedding day, vacation or major promotion at your job. The light and exuberant experience of being momentarily satisfied is what causes us to pursue these moments over and over again. Whether we realize it or not, we default to doing whatever makes us happiest in the moment. Without getting too philosophical here, even when we discipline ourselves to accomplish something difficult, it's a choice we make to actively pursue what we most want to do in the moment—even if it's not particularly our favorite thing.

> All men seek happiness. This is without exception. Whatever different means they employ, they all tend to this end. The cause of some going to war, and of others avoiding it, is the same desire in both, attended with different views. The will never takes the least step but to this object. This is the motive of every action of every man, even of those who hang themselves.[2]

Happiness can also be a general feeling, how we wish others well or how we decide to pursue different avenues in life. We break from relationships because they're not making us happy anymore. We wish people all the happiness in the world. We tell loved ones that we just want them to be happy. We leave careers because we believe we'd be happier working somewhere else. All of those choices are motivated by the belief that there is something better, someplace other, than the place we are in.

In some ways, we're like the character played by Will Smith in the movie *The Pursuit of Happyness*, a down-on-his-luck single father who frantically tries to earn a job at an investment firm in hopes of providing a better life for his young son. For Smith's character, happiness would've been a steady supply of life's basic necessities, like food, clothing and shelter. For those of us whose basic needs have been attained and maintained (and probably taken for granted), our wants get elevated to the category of "essential."

When that happens, we exhaustively try to achieve something that will bring a greater state of well-being. We do whatever it takes for more pleasurable items and more satisfying experiences, hoping that just this one time, they'll be more than momentary.

But is that really how God intended for us to live? Hanging by a thread from one elusive moment to the next? Our sense of peace, hope and well-being dependent upon a series of fortunate events? Isn't this what Jesus came to deliver us out of?

The Contrast

What people really want, and what they typically mean when they talk about the pursuit of happiness, is really the attainment of joy. The difference between the two may not *feel* incredibly different, but they are different, although not entirely opposed to one another.

> The best news in the world is that there is no conflict between your greatest possible happiness and God's perfect holiness. Being satisfied with all that God is for you in Jesus magnifies him as the greatest treasure and brings you more joy—eternal, infinite joy—than any other delight ever could.[3]

Joy is sometimes defined as a feeling of great happiness.[4] But the beauty and effectiveness of joy is that it moves beyond mere feeling, while never ignoring that the emotions of happiness can be good and God-given.

> Looking to Jesus, the founder and perfecter of our faith, who for the joy that was set before him endured the cross, despising the shame, and is seated at the right hand of the throne of God. (Heb. 12:2)

The writer of Hebrews gives us a working definition of joy from the perspective of the most joyful person who ever walked the earth, Jesus Christ. It was because of the joy Jesus had in obeying His father and fulfilling the work necessary for the redemption of mankind that He was able to endure something as horrific as the cross. For Jesus, joy consisted of more than momentary lightness and positivity. If it didn't, the Bible wouldn't describe Him the way it does, like in Isaiah 53:3 where the prophet says, "He was despised and rejected by men; a man of sorrows, and acquainted with grief; and as one from whom men hide their faces he was despised, and we esteemed him not."

Or on the night before His crucifixion, when Jesus was in agony over what would shortly transpire: "And being in an agony he prayed more earnestly; and his sweat became like great drops of blood falling down to the ground" (Luke 22:44).

And yet, in the midst of the single greatest sacrifice since the creation of the world, there was a joy that ran deeper. It's fair to say from the text that Jesus was not "happy" during the height of His suffering and sacrifice, but His joy was of a deeper, richer and altogether more infinite quality than any temporary feeling of relief could have provided Him. It was "for" and "because of" joy that the "unhappy" circumstances leading up to and through His death couldn't diminish.

Happiness is always dependent on the "if." "If" this happens, then I'll be happy. Joy, on the other hand, is always "because of." "Because of" this, I'm already content. For example, one might say, "If I just get this job promotion, it will make me happy." And that may be true, in the moment.

But joy exists outside of the push and pull of present circumstances or fate. Joy is this: "Whether I get this job promotion or not, I trust that God has my future in His hands and it's this never-changing truth that will be a constant source of gladness."

Happiness hangs in the balance of realization, but joy remains resolutely grounded on what's already been realized. In other words, happiness has to continually be earned, like a person working for wages. If he works, he earns, and he can take temporary comfort in those things that his wages earn him.

But joy is a gift bought and paid for, completely dependent on a giver whose gifts are eternal and unfading. In a nutshell, joy is grace.

> For by grace you have been saved through faith. And this is not your own doing; it is the gift of God, not a result of works, so that no one may boast. (Eph. 2:8–9)

Joy is also a guarantee, because the Holy Spirit seals the source of joy, the gospel, in our hearts.

> In him you also, when you heard the word of truth, the gospel of your salvation, and believed in him, were sealed with the promised Holy Spirit, who is the guarantee of our inheritance until we acquire possession of it, to the praise of his glory. (Eph. 1:13–14)

The apostle Peter adds to what Paul said by calling this message of good news a "living hope":

> According to his great mercy, He has caused us to be born again to a living hope through the resurrection of Jesus Christ from the dead, to an inheritance that is imperishable, undefiled, and unfading, kept in heaven for you, who by God's power are being guarded through faith for a salvation ready to be revealed in the last time. (1 Peter 1:3–5)

According to Peter, the cause for our hope, and the subsequent joy that follows, is our new birth in Christ through the effective power of His resurrection from the dead. What we receive is an everlasting inheritance, like God literally writing our names on His will, stating we will receive an infinite supply of riches that He's guarding through our faith by His power. So the full measure of those riches are still forthcoming, but we get a portion of them now through the Holy Spirit's sanctifying work in our lives.

This is part of the "already/not yet" reality for the Christian. We've been given so much, and so much is still yet to come. Christ has provided justification and sanctification, but we await the day of our glorification, when our joy will be uninhibited by our natural inclination toward earthly pleasures.

Our Gravitational Pull

In the 2013 sci-fi thriller *Gravity*, two astronauts, played by Sandra Bullock and George Clooney (I mean, why can't astronauts be good looking, right?), are sent on a mission to service the Hubble telescope. While making repairs during their spacewalk, a Russian missile strike destroys the station and their ship and leaves Sandra fighting for her life and to get back to Earth. Everyone she loves and everything she knows is down on that big, blue globe. Her only hope is to get her capsule through the atmosphere and land safely. There's a lot more, but I won't spoil it for you.

But that's just like us in a spiritual sense. The things of earth pull at us and draw us back in. We gravitate toward things of less eternal value. They're not necessarily bad things. But we can't make them ultimate things, either. Tim Keller, pastor of Redeemer Presbyterian Church in Manhattan, writes in his book *Counterfeit Gods*,

> The human heart is an idol factory that takes good things like a successful career, love, material possessions, even family, and turns them into ultimate things. Our hearts deify them as the center of our lives, because, we think, they

can give us significance and security, safety and fulfillment, if we attain them.[5]

What are the ultimate things in your life? What kind of story would your life tell us if we took a casual look at your bank statement, what's parked inside your garage or the things you have hanging in your closet?

C.S. Lewis famously said, "Aim at heaven and you will get earth thrown in: aim at earth and you will get neither."[6]

The problem is that we have a sin nature that is going to trick our minds into believing that things of a lesser glory are most glorious. Before Christ, none of us aimed at heaven. None of us! As self-lovers, the only aim of our hearts and minds was to pursue those things that gave us the greatest amount of earthbound pleasure. But when Christ saved us, our eyes were opened to an otherworldly kind of love and affection that was universally different to what we had ever known. And that's because it was a love that had its origins outside of our world, until it entered the world through one man, Jesus Christ. Paul tells us in the book of Romans:

> For while we were still weak, at the right time Christ died for the ungodly. For one will scarcely die for a righteous person—though perhaps for a good person one would dare even to die— but God shows His love for us in that while we were still sinners, Christ died for us. (5:6–8)

We all make sacrifices. We work tirelessly at jobs, spend endless hours at school, put years and years into relationships, and those are all noble pursuits that bring varying degrees of happy moments. Interestingly, Jesus sacrificed Himself for something far more important than happiness. He sacrificed everything for God's glory, His joy and our peace with God. He accomplished it while living what many would call a very unhappy life. He also did it without complaining, because His desires were not wrapped up in the things of this world. His lack of earthly possessions and creature comforts, and his maligned reputation, never caused Him to grumble to His heavenly Father.

After someone had come up to Jesus declaring that he would follow Him wherever He would go, Jesus replied, "Foxes have holes, and birds of the air have nests, but the Son of Man has nowhere to lay his head" (Luke 9:58).

Jesus was saying, "Be prepared for the cost that comes with following Me. Understand that I didn't come to earth to inherit more of it, but to call people whom God has chosen to inherit something that neither moth nor rust destroys." (see Matt. 6:20)

Dietrich Bonhoeffer said, "When Christ calls a man, he bids him come and die."[7]

I'm not sure we see such a clear correlation between dying and delight in our current cultural sphere. When we think of delight, we think of something closer to decadence. We think of having those things that fulfill the greatest desires our earthly appetites can conjure up. In the spiritual sense, dying is the removal of a desire that has descended to the formation of an idol.

I'm going to be honest here by saying that I don't mind having some nice things. Although not extravagant, I like where I live, I like the food I eat and I like my furnace that is currently blowing out warm air, since it's five degrees outside. I don't know if all my happiness is wrapped up in these things, but if they were absent or even less conveniently at my disposal, I wonder if I'd be spending my energy pursuing the acquisition of some version of them. It's a good thing to pursue shelter, food and warmth, but are these basic necessities the primary focus and drive of our hearts?

This cumulative effect of assumption and expectation is what leads many of us to a warped sense of entitlement. Because many of us were given so much and expected to contribute so little, we grew up with the expectation that everybody else must owe us everything as well.

In the bestselling biography *Into the Wild*, author Jon Krakauer writes, "It is easy, when you are young, to believe that what you desire is no less than what you deserve, to assume that if you want something badly enough, it is your God-given right to have it."[8]

Oddly, because of this, it seems like we've found ourselves in a generation that has little practical understanding of what Christ's fully bought-and-paid-for work on the cross really means for us. If we've never had the experience of working for something, it might be hard for us to muster any sort of gratefulness for yet another free gift given to us, even if it is by our Savior.

Preaching that gratitude for the gift of salvation is the ultimate defense against grumbling becomes an interesting proposition, given the sense of entitlement under which many people under fifty have grown up. Why shouldn't salvation be a gift? After all, I deserve it, don't I? Haven't I been told how special I am since the day I was born? Haven't I succeeded at everything I've tried, been given a trophy for every effort ever made and told, "Good job, buddy!" for any energy I've expended toward almost anything? Why would salvation be something I shouldn't be deserving of?

While the older and "greater" generation may have struggled greatly with the temptation of works righteousness, the current one struggles with the opposite idea: that they're already inherently righteous, infinitely deserving and therefore don't need to work for it at all. In other words, if legalism tells us that salvation can only be earned through good works, entitlement believes it's already good enough to not have to work at all. As the legalist will work hard to be justified, the entitled feel they were already born that way. In the end, it all funnels down to the same thing, which is that the payment made by the blood of Jesus is for both the self-earner and the self-righteous and therefore the only way to be accepted by God for salvation. Interestingly, in both cases, it still boils down to good old fashioned legalism. It's still something "other" than Jesus.

In his book *Jesus + Nothing = Everything*, Tullian Tchividjan says, "Legalism breeds a sense of entitlement that turns us into complainers."[9]

If it's true that "Jesus paid it all" like the old hymn tells us, then it means the only outcome for anyone living a self-earning or self-righteous existence will be exhaustion. The intention of Jesus was for something entirely different. Jesus says in the book of John, "The thief comes only to steal and kill and destroy. I came that they may have life and have it abundantly. I am the good shepherd. The good shepherd lays down his life for the sheep" (10:10–11).

With the death of Jesus came the possibility for an abundant life. What kind of abundance?

An abundance of love

See what kind of love the Father has given to us, that we should be called children of God; and so we are. (1 John 3:1)

An abundance of grace

For from his fullness we have all received, grace upon grace. (John 1:16)

An abundance of mercy

The steadfast love of the LORD never ceases; his mercies never come to an end; they are new every morning; great is your faithfulness. (Lam. 3:22–23)

An abundance of hope

We always thank God, the Father of our Lord Jesus Christ, when we pray for you, since we heard of your faith in Christ Jesus and of the love that you have for all the saints, because of the hope laid up for you in heaven. (Col. 1:3–5)

The legalist says, "I need to work hard to buy these back!" while the entitled one says, "I already have it all because I deserve it." Both are damning distortions of the oldest lie ever told, which is that we don't need Jesus to have peace with God.

Peace with God comes down to the inexhaustible work of joy and salvation that Christ accomplished for us on the cross and through His resurrection. It's the gospel work that declares, "You couldn't earn it, so I earned it for you so that you could rest in Me." It's the gospel work that declares, "You weren't born with it, so I died for you so you could be born again and never lose it."

Defend Your Joy

Complaining comes surfacing to our mouths and sliding out of our lips when we're not defending the blood-bought joy provided for us by Jesus Christ. The reason we need a defense is because we're not battling against flesh and blood (see Eph. 6) but against an enemy and thief whose offensive aim is to steal and kill and destroy (see John 10). The apostle Peter tells us we have "an inheritance that is imperishable, undefiled, and unfading, kept in heaven for you, who by God's power are being guarded through faith for a salvation ready to be revealed in the last time" (I Peter 1:4–5). It's our faith in Jesus by the power of God that allows us to defend and delight in our joy because of God's unfailing provision in Christ.

Yet even though our exhausting pursuit of happiness is over-come by Christ's inexhaustible work of joy, it doesn't mean that we don't have a fight on our hands to make sure this finished work stays finished in spite of the deceitfulness of our hearts and minds! Is that a contradiction? How do I stop pursuing one thing (happiness) but work hard to defend another (joy) without becom-ing a tired, frustrated wage earner? Won't this be the very thing that leads me to becoming a greater grumbler than I already am? The short answer is, no! If part of our complaining comes from our short-fused attempts at pursuing temporal happinesses, then working toward resting in God's joy-filled grace will ultimate-ly lead us to grace-filled rest. It's what we sometimes refer to as "hard, but good work." Am I talking in circles here? Maybe this illustration will help.

In 2015, my wife Melissa and I celebrated twenty years of mar-riage. Like all couples, we've experienced some delightful ups as well as a few dramatic downs, and yet in hindsight we've seen a very clear stream of God's grace that's sustained us through the never-ending layers of life stages and seasons that we continue to wade through.

One of the things God has blessed our marriage with is trust. I trust Melissa without question, and her trust in me is the same. In all of our years together, which has included quite a bit of travel by yours truly, I never once worried about her being unfaithful to me, and vice versa. There's never been a time when I doubted wheth-er she still loved me and I her. At the risk of painting too smug a picture of our marriage, let me assure you of the many times she's wanted to clobber me and hasn't had the slightest bit of hesitation telling me so. It hasn't always been a Disney movie, and we unarguably struggle in many areas that other couples don't give a second thought to. In spite of all that, and here's my critical point, I've never felt burdened or compelled to try to earn her love, but that doesn't mean I don't do everything I can to show her my love.

In the years I spent on the road before cell phones, sometimes a day or two would pass by when I wouldn't talk to my wife because I couldn't get to a phone booth (phone booths were these tall, metal contraptions that you'd stand inside to put money into a big, square box which would then allow you to make a phone call). When I finally called, the question inevitably came up as to why I hadn't been able to contact her for the last couple of days. But her question wasn't accusatory, it was born out of concern. She knew she could trust me, she just missed me. It was the same for me whenever I tried to reach her but kept getting the answering machine (another archaic device). Never once did I think she loved me less if I failed to contact her. I called because I wanted to hear her voice and hear all about what she was doing while I was gone. This is something that's only continued to increase over the years.

Because of the love and trust that's been built up and cultivated over the years, it's a joy for me to do things for her that I know will please her and bring her joy. I don't think for a minute that if I don't do something, she will stop loving me and run off with another man, but there would be something wrong if I never sacrificed anything for her. If I spent all of my time only pursuing my own needs and wants without ever considering hers, what would that say about my love for her? What would you conclude? Probably that I didn't love her very much and that my interest in pleasing myself far exceeded my interest in pleasing her. You'd rightly describe me as selfish, and certainly not as a servant.

But what would you think if you saw me working hard to sacrificially love and please my wife? Would you think I ever look tired? Occasionally, sure, because sacrifice requires hard, intentional work. But what would be the thing you'd most likely see?

You'd see my wife's joy. Which would then be my joy.

In the same way, our "doing" needs to come on the heels of what Jesus has done. We don't work hard to earn, we work hard because of what's already been earned for us. When that happens and the gospel, in all of its gargantuan and glorious goodness becomes our greatest cause for joy, our pursuits then became redefined and redirected. And the words that come out of our mouths won't be a series of complaints due to disappointment over unfulfilled expectations. Instead, we'll enjoy whatever happiness God gives us because we see a greater, more lasting, more eternal joy that gives meaning to our pleasures and purpose to our pain. Paul provides us with this great hope when he says, "And we know that for those who love God all things work together for good, for those who are called according to his purpose. For those whom he foreknew he also predestined to be conformed to the image of his Son, in order that he might be the firstborn among many brothers" (Rom. 8:28–29).

When people used to ask me as a kid what my favorite day of the year was, I would always say Christmas Eve. Why? Because the next day was Christmas! Christmas Eve was the one day of the year when I could adequately anticipate the greatest day of the year. There was nothing that could happen on Christmas Eve, short of death, that could take away the excitement I had for what was coming the next day.

Any sort of task or chore my parents gave me was transformed into a happiness because a bigger joy was hovering over it. Clean my room? No problem, Mom. Help my sister? I'll get right on it, Dad. There was nothing that could diminish my joy because my eye was placed squarely on the object that contained every ounce of it. There was no work, no pursuit that I found myself crushed under the weight of, because for that one day I had a vision of how much I knew I had to be grateful for. So I worked with inexhaustible joy.

This is the good work of God that He accomplishes in our pain and through our pleasures, to provide us with an inexhaustible joy that comes with being conformed into the image of Christ. It's this work of grace that allows our grumbling to finally grind to an abrupt halt.

Reflection Questions:

1. How would you define the difference between happiness and joy? When things that provide happiness come to an end, what kind of response do you have?

2. What is God's ultimate "inexhaustible work of joy"? What are some ways this combats complaining when applied to your life?

3. How do we work toward joy in a way that brings gratefulness to our hearts?

6

THE UNDESERVED GRACE OF GRATEFULNESS

*"But if it is by grace, it is no longer on the basis of works;
otherwise grace would no longer be grace."*

Romans 11:6

*"The whole life of man until he is converted to Christ
is a ruinous labyrinth of wanderings."*

—John Calvin

Some Horribly Academic Definitions:

Undeserved: *Not warranted, merited or earned.*[1]
Grace: *Unmerited divine assistance given humans for
their regeneration or sanctification.*[2]
Gratefulness: *Appreciation for benefits received.*[3]

In Victor Hugo's *Les Misérables*, one of the greatest novels of the nineteenth century, we're given a beautiful, scandalous picture of grace. The story's hero, Jean Valjean, is released on parole after serving a nineteen-year prison sentence for stealing a loaf of bread. Upon release, he struggles to find employment, due to his damaged social status. One night, the Bishop of Digne shows kindness to Valjean by providing him with food and shelter, but Valjean returns the bishop's good graces by stealing his silver in the middle of the night, proving that jail time did little to reform his depraved heart. Valjean is soon caught, but in another turn of kindness, the bishop tells the authorities that the silver was given to Valjean as a gift. They release him, but this time Valjean is so humbled by the bishop's gracious response that it prompts him to embark on a brand new life.

For the Christian, this classic scene is a picture of the gospel. It is a picture of how our response to God's grace crystallizes our hearts into ever flowing fountains of gratefulness. At one point, we were all like Valjean, prisoners serving a life sentence for crimes both great and small. Even when given the opportunity to get out and do better for ourselves, we found that our sin nature held us back from acquiring even our basic spiritual needs.

Instead, we remained malnourished and starving for the true spiritual nutrients that remained out of our grasp. It wasn't until Christ showered His undeserved grace on us that our souls were given the sustenance and substance necessary to grow into and thrive in the kind of grateful life God had originally designed for Adam. Like the Bishop of Digne, God didn't have to show us grace, but when He did, our lives became stories of gratefulness.

We struggle when confronted with grace because it feels raw, uncomfortable and category-defying. Our natural inclination is to be shocked and then offended by the selfless nature of it. It's difficult to fathom, on both an intellectual and spiritual level, why someone would want to give us something that we didn't work for and therefore don't deserve.

Grace humbles us. Our visceral reaction to it shines an unveiled light on our desperate need for it. The contrast between our reception and rejection of grace is described beautifully and poignantly in Luke's Gospel.

> One of the criminals who were hanged railed at him, saying, "Are you not the Christ? Save yourself and us!" But the other rebuked him, saying, "Do you not fear God, since you are under the same sentence of condemnation? And we indeed justly, for we are receiving the due reward of our deeds; but this man has done nothing wrong." And he said, "Jesus, remember me when you come into your kingdom." And he said to him, "Truly, I say to you, today you will be with me in Paradise." (Luke 23:39–43)

Notice what happens here. The first criminal rails at Jesus, complaining to Him that He should use His divine powers, if He has any, to deliver them from their irrevocable predicament. He's saying, "If You are who You say You are, get me off this cross so that I can go back to being who I am!" Sadly, this convicted thief only saw Jesus as a means to his own ends. He wanted to be saved from the cross, never realizing that the cross was the only thing that could save him from himself and God.

The other criminal never asked to be delivered from the cross. He knew his fate was death and that it was death that he deserved. His greatest need wasn't to be saved from the cross, but by the cross, and to be remembered by Jesus. In one of the most tender moments in all of Scripture, Jesus replies to him by saying He'll do more than remember him, He'll remain with him for all eternity.

How often do we share the sentiment of the first criminal, voicing the same kind of heart? We don't want to die to our sins with Christ, we want Him to lead us only so far as to help us remain the lords of our own lives. And when He doesn't grant our wishes, we rail at and rebuke Him in our angry, entitled hearts.

Though Scripture doesn't record the reaction of the redeemed criminal who received grace and forgiveness, we can know with absolute certainty that his heart was overflowing with gratefulness.

Death had lost its sting, because the one dying next to him would defeat it in three days. This providential moment of God's undeserved grace produced a gratefulness in him that still exists today as he praises and glorifies Jesus face to face for all eternity.

God's grace is not only undeserved, but it's also unwanted, meaning it was actually done against our natural wills. Paul quotes the prophet Isaiah in Romans 3:11, reminding us that "no one understands; no one seeks for God." Before God's grace transformed our hearts, our hearts didn't want anything to do with His transforming grace. You begin to understand why this is when you read about the state of our souls before Christ redeemed them.

> And you were dead in the trespasses and sins in which you once walked, following the course of this world, following the prince of the power of the air, the spirit that is now at work in the sons of disobedience—among whom we all once lived in the passions of our flesh, carrying out the desires of the body and the mind, and were by nature children of wrath, like the rest of mankind. But God, being rich in mercy, because of the great love with which He loved us, even when we were dead in our trespasses, made us alive together with Christ—by grace you have been saved. (Eph. 2:1–5)

It's that part about *once living in the passions of our flesh* that makes gratefulness to God impossible until the grace of God makes it possible. We are conceived as people who are against the loving kindness of God. King David the psalmist writes, "Behold, I was brought forth in iniquity, and in sin did my mother conceive me" (Ps. 51:5).

We are inherently ungrateful because we can't be grateful for something we are predisposed from birth to not want to receive.

That's why grace is the only thing that has the effective power to create true gratefulness in the hearts of all those who trust in Jesus.

We've probably all lived through the frustration of seeing somebody in need, trying to help them, and watching them inexplicably refuse our generosity. Not only that, but they become angry or offended that help was even offered. Pride blinds us from seeing that we need something to make us see!

Growing up, my daughter was the definition of an independent kid. Anytime she was trying to learn something new, she was determined to figure it out and accomplish it all by herself. She was inevitably driven to frustration because she refused to receive any instruction, which many times would lead to her give up on the project completely. If she only would have let us help her in those moments, she would have experienced our grace and even learned to be grateful for it in the process. Shoot, it would've made us more grateful, too!

Grace That Reaches

It's hard to find a story as infused with grace as that of the apostle Paul. A Pharisee of the strictest order in Israel, Paul had made it his life's quest to abolish this growing sect of people who were following and gathering in the name of a crucified religious rebel called Jesus. He spent his time locking up and murdering anyone who was trying to spread the news about this blasphemer. And then this happened:

> Now as he went on his way, he approached Damascus, and suddenly a light from heaven shone around him. And falling to the ground he heard a voice saying to him, "Saul, Saul, why are you persecuting me?" And he said, "Who are you, Lord?" And he said, "I am Jesus, whom you are persecuting. But rise and enter the city, and you will be told what

you are to do." The men who were traveling with him stood speechless, hearing the voice but seeing no one. Saul rose from the ground, and although his eyes were opened, he saw nothing. So they led him by the hand and brought him into Damascus. And for three days he was without sight, and neither ate nor drank. (Acts 9:3–9)

You'll find few, if any, conversion experiences that are as dramatic as Paul's. On his way to Damascus to arrest followers of Jesus, Jesus visits Paul first and causes this proud, devout Pharisee to collapse under the weight of His heavenly light. Jesus doesn't get into a lot of back-and-forth banter, but asks him a very direct question, which Paul answers with another question, "Who are you, Lord?" Jesus answers by telling Paul that his murderous acts have been done against Him only and that he needs to enter the city for further instructions. It's interesting to note that Paul leaves his conversion experience physically blind, but spiritually seeing for the first time.

So why Paul? Surely God had a number of other men he could've chosen to carry out the work of spreading the news of His kingdom throughout the world. Why choose an opponent, an enemy, a renowned rebel who'd been on a crusade against the cause of Christ? Well, that's where our thinking starts to get a bit faulty.

Before Christ rescued us, we were all opponents, enemies and rebels of Christ. In our minds, Paul probably appears to be a greater antagonist to Jesus than we ever were, but in reality, we once were just as against Him as Paul. Paul didn't believe in Him, didn't love Him, didn't accept Him as the truth, and had a heart that was hardened against the gospel.

It's true that Paul did greater overall damage to the early church, due to his zealous and violent adherence to Jewish law, but personally, he needed the same amount of God's grace as each one of us do: all of it. What Jesus did for Paul is what He does for each one of us whom He saves: He reaches down, exposes our sin with the light of truth and then raises us up as new creatures to send us on mission to proclaim a message about Himself. It's the most gracious act of love imaginable, revealing to us our depraved hearts so that we can ask in repentance to receive forgiven hearts instead.

Like Paul, we didn't ask to be reached out to. God chose us before the foundation of the world to be His predestined sons and daughters. As He clearly laid out to the Ephesian church, "For by grace you have been saved through faith. And this is not your own doing; it is the gift of God, not a result of works, so that no one may boast" (Eph. 2:8–9).

And then in the book of Romans, "for all have sinned and fall short of the glory of God, and are justified by his grace as a gift, through the redemption that is in Christ Jesus" (3:23–24).

It's this "gift-only" nature of grace that makes it the glorious unearned reality that it is. If it is anything less, it wouldn't be as far reaching, and if it was any less far reaching, none of us would ever have a chance of receiving it.

Every year, I buy my daughter a birthday present. She might disagree with me on this, but there's nothing really forcing me to buy her a gift. I do it because I love her, and I want to give her something to commemorate and celebrate the day she was born. But here's the thing: she only receives a birthday gift from me because every year, before her birthday, I choose to buy one for her. That's the concept of a gift. It's completely dependent on the decision of the one who decides to give or not give it. The receiver's responsibility is to receive the gift, but they can't receive something until the giver decides to give them something to receive. Ideally, they receive a gift with gratitude because they know that it was the decision of the giver to gift them something they didn't earn. If it was something they earned, it wouldn't be a gift, it would be a payment. In the case of gifting, the only one who pays anything for the gift is the giver.

It's with this understanding of God's free gift of grace that our response as Christians is one of growing gratefulness. Growing, because the more we get to know God, the more we see how great His grace was in giving us the gift of Christ, and therefore we become progressively more grateful with the passing of time as we gain a deeper and richer appreciation of the magnitude of the gift. In our sanctification, we're becoming more aware of and grieved by our sin, while simultaneously becoming more grateful for God's grace through Christ, which humbles us to be more like Christ.

Expressing gratitude is our sanctification against grumbling. It's visible proof that God's grace is working in and through us. Am I saying that unbelievers are never thankful for things? Of course not, but the question is, to whom are they ultimately thankful? Without Christ, it can only go as deep as a person, or something as impersonal as fate or dumb luck. For the believer, gratefulness is grace-infused. It comes as the result of a heart change that causes our internal gaze to become reoriented to the person and work of Jesus.

The Corinthian church of the New Testament was a mess, sinking in the quagmire of everything from quarreling, jealousy, anger, hostility, slander, gossip, conceit and disorder, to issues of impurity and sexual immorality. So Paul writes two letters to rebuke, correct and firmly but lovingly call them back to biblical, repentant, Christ-centered living.

As part of his disciplinary direction and tone, he also reminds the Corinthians of what they have to be thankful for in Christ. "But thanks be to God, who gives us the victory through our Lord Jesus Christ" (1 Cor. 15:57).

Notice the manner and structure of how he thanks God. He doesn't just offer up an ambiguous "Thanks, God," but he states the reason and motivation for why God is worthy to be thanked. The object is Christ's victory on the cross.

Then, in Second Corinthians 4:15, he mentions one of the purposes of divine grace, and why it is so vital for the Christian. "For it is all for your sake, so that as grace extends to more and more people it may increase thanksgiving, to the glory of God."

It's God's grace that is responsible for the increase, for giving us hearts that become more and more immersed in thankfulness. If you've been in the church for even a short amount of time, you begin to see the evidence of this in some of those around you.

One of my elders, Dave, is one of the most thankful people I have ever met. His words and even the tone of his words emanate a grace and gratefulness that have come from years of faithfully walking with and serving Jesus. Dave's primary, full-time job is traveling overseas to remote regions in places like Romania and Mongolia to train church planting pastors who don't have access to the seminary training that we have the privilege of accessing in the West. Like most missionaries, Dave has stories that range from the hopeful to the heartbreaking, of pastors and people who endure not only persecution, but also lack of food, shelter, medical care and other common necessities. The one thing that always strikes me about Dave is how he never seems weighed down by the challenges and never stops attesting to how well he sees the grace of God working in the minutiae. It's not that he tries to sugarcoat anything, either. He's open and honest about the struggles, downturns and near-impossible odds that continue to plague the pastors he ministers to, but he also believes in the infinite reach of God's grace. Because of that, he never stops being thankful and because of that, God is glorified.

Grace That Keeps

Do you possess this grace that reaches in and keeps you growing in God's gratefulness? If you're in Christ, the Bible says you do, actually: "For from his fullness we have all received, grace upon grace. For the law was given through Moses; grace and truth came through Jesus Christ" (John 1:16-17).

So what do we do with this grace upon grace we have all received? Since it's grace, is there anything to "do" with it, or is it just conceptual? Isn't the very nature and definition of grace that it's unmerited, that it causes us to rest in something already accomplished and finished for us? Absolutely! Faith alone, in Christ alone, by grace alone are the biblical pillars of the Christian faith that the reformers fought to keep central to the church.

The great sixteenth-century reformer Martin Luther famously said, "We are saved by faith alone, but the faith that saves is never alone."

So then, is grace supposed to motivate us toward something?

Paul tells the Ephesians, "For we are his workmanship, created in Christ Jesus for good works, which God prepared beforehand, that we should walk in them" (Eph. 2:10).

So if it's by grace we've been saved and not by works, what does it mean to have been created for good works in Christ Jesus? Practically, it means that God made us to be ambassadors and representatives of the good work He already accomplished through

His son Jesus. Because grace keeps me secure in Christ, I have total freedom to work on behalf of Christ.

As I mentioned earlier, in the summer of 2010 God called my wife, our teenage daughter and me to a small university town in central Ohio. The town felt idyllic in all the ways you might imagine a small town could be. The streets were lined with luscious greens trees and beautiful Cape Cod-style homes. There was a park with a bandshell, an ice cream stand, a small lake and a quaint little brook that ran through the grassy knolls. At night when you looked out your window you could see your lawn come alive with the glow of fireflies blinking on and off like Christmas tree lights. On my first day of work, I rode my bicycle down the tree-lined streets with a soft, balmy breeze blowing gently against my skin. It felt like something from a novel. Until the first storm broke. We'd never seen anything like it. The thunder was almost deafening, the lightning almost blinding. The trees looked like they were going to be uprooted, and everybody kept talking about these things called tornadoes that I thought were mythical tunnels of wind from *The Wizard of Oz*. I remember the three of us lying on the bed upstairs, staring out the window, wondering if we were going to survive. Being from California, we were used to earthquakes, where the house would shake for a few seconds and then you'd be back to business as usual. This felt a little more serious. Like the wrath of God.

But eventually we all got up, went back downstairs and got back to our lives. The storm still raged on around us, but we were safe and secure in our house. We could've stayed in bed shivering and quivering until the storm passed, but we realized we were perfectly capable of carrying on with life because whoever had built the house had done so with the knowledge that it needed to withstand summer storms. And it did! The house had been created to do the very thing it was accomplishing: to house and shelter us against the brutal elements of nature.

This is a picture of how God's grace works in our lives. I had nothing to do with the construction of the house we were renting at the time. I was given a key by the owner and invited in. Because of that, I benefited from all the amenities that the home provided. I was free to simply live, work and enjoy.

Because of the gospel of grace, we are free to move about and accomplish the work that God has given us. In Christ, we are kept securely inside something immovable and steadfast that allows us to work freely with confidence and assurance.

Paul exhorts the Colossian church with these words: "If then you have been raised with Christ, seek the things that are above, where Christ is, seated at the right hand of God. Set your minds on things that are above, not on things that are on earth. For you have died, and your life is hidden with Christ in God. When Christ who is your life appears, then you also will appear with him in glory" (Col. 3:1–4).

This gives us a short but fairly comprehensive picture of how our lives are to be lived out before God, and what awaits us.

First off, Paul gives us a strategy for our minds. He's saying, if your mind has been renewed by the saving power of Christ, then rest your thoughts, your concentration and your focus on those things that only exist where Christ exists. Things of an eternal, nontemporal nature, the greatest of these being Christ himself.

Then he reminds us of our transformation, that we died to our sins the way Christ died for all sin, and it's because of this death that we experience a new life that is now hidden securely in

The apostle John warns and encourages us, "And the world is passing away along with its desires, but whoever does the will of God abides forever" (1 John 2:17).

Jesus Paid Some of It

One of the largely unspoken benefits of being a kid is that you never have to pay for anything. Part of the job of being a parent is taking care of your kids' needs because they aren't in a life position to take care of anything themselves. What this translates to is that parents get the privilege of footing the bill for almost everything. To be fair, there are occasions when kids actually do pay for things, but it still tends to come from you (allowance) or somebody else (gift). The standard rule is that parents provide, and by providing they're fulfilling the role God has given them to care for their families.

Never once did my mom place a bill next to my plate after serving dinner and say "I'll take care of that whenever you're ready, honey." I don't ever remember my dad dropping me off at school in the morning and saying "Let's see, the fare from our house to the school parking lot comes to $17.59, buckaroo." It would've been shocking and outrageous. And actually kind of hilarious, if truth be told.

Parents pay for everything because it's their responsibility to care for the needs of their children to the best of their ability, and they do it most of the time with almost zero appreciation, acknowledgement or applause whatsoever. It's just assumed and expected.

There's a reason why kids have to be told over and over again to say the words "thank you." Those two words don't come naturally because most kids have never had to earn anything which might cause them to be thankful for something they *didn't* earn, much less something that *couldn't* be earned, such as salvation.

the life of the resurrected Christ. But our lives don't simply exist in the immobile environment of an incubator. We wait for a future hope, a greater end glory that will appear when Christ appears.

So what does a mind that seeks and sets its mind on things above look like? First off, it puts to death earthly things (see Col. 3:5). Paul lists sexual immorality, impurity, passion, evil desire and covetousness as the reasons for which the wrath of God is coming (see 3:5–6). Although at first it may seem like a strange connection to make, if you were to dig into the soil of these earthly things, you'd find the fuel that drives the engine of our grumbling and complaining. Whenever you spend time giving life to earthly things, the aroma of death that fills the air in your heart will give way to a bitter tongue.

Secondly, in response to putting to death those things characteristic of our old life, Paul instructs the church to put on "compassionate hearts, kindness, humility, meekness, and patience, bearing with one another and, if one has a complaint against another, forgiving each other; as the Lord has forgiven you, so you also must forgive. And above all these put on love, which binds everything together in perfect harmony" (3:12–14).

What we have here is the most intentional and active counterresponse to complaining. God tells us to put to death earthly things, yes, but part of the death process happens when we actively replace the earthly with the heavenly. If we only put to death earthly things, we'd be like a runner training for a marathon who only concentrates on eliminating unhealthy foods but fails to replace them with healthy ones! After not very long, energy will be depleted and endurance will be lost.

The Christian allows grace to be the fuel that produces the fruit of his or her life. We put on the character attributes of Christ, and pray that our motivation to be more like Him comes from our abiding love for Him, not selfish compulsion.

Let's discuss practicalities and possibilities.

Reflection Questions

1.   Take a minute to define the grace of God. Have you lacked an understanding of what grace truly is? Compile a short list of some of the ways God's grace has been evident in your life.

2.   Is expressing gratefulness to God a daily part of your life? Name some things you can be thankful for right in this moment.

3.   How does being grateful cause us to see the grace of God more greatly? How will this affect how we live?

7

AFFECTED BY COMPLAINING

*"If you do well, will you not be accepted? And if you do not do well,
sin is crouching at the door. Its desire is for you,
but you must rule over it."*

Genesis 4:7

"Be killing sin, or it will be killing you."

—John Owen

I t's been said that human beings are creatures of habit. We like the stability that comes with doing the same things over and over again. There's a part of us that enjoys going mindlessly through the paces of life. I know this personally because I can become irritable if I get too far out of a daily routine. I see the effects of this most clearly when I travel. My mornings aren't the same. No comfy couch for my daily devotions. No French press for my coffee. My familiar workspace is unavailable. Ministry appointments are on hold. Dinner with my wife doesn't happen. Connections with friends are impossible. My much-loved bed is miles away. I realize these are first world problems I'm describing here, but I'm still affected by them, and after a while I start complaining about them.

Complaining is a habitual thing for us. It's something that is such a regular part of our vocabulary that the idea of actually breaking the pattern of it in our lives might seem unrealistic and overwhelming. Think of how many conversations begin with responding to the question of how we're doing with a sigh, shrug and story of all the things that are going wrong this week for us. We do it without even thinking about it.

Benjamin Franklin said that it's easier to prevent bad habits than to break them, but I'm approaching complaining as something that needs to be broken, with the assumption that we haven't prevented it from becoming a habit in the first place.

First off, let's accept the fact that because of our fallen natures we're always going to be prone to complaining. I can't begin to tell you the countless times I complained to someone about writing this book on complaining! Some might argue that even writing a book on complaining is nothing more than the opportunity to complain about what big complainers we are!

Secondly, not all complaining is necessarily bad, as we pointed out in earlier chapters. There are times when it's a good and godly thing to say, "This isn't the way it's supposed to be and I don't like it!" Mistreatment, bad health, financial downturns, family struggles and relational disunity are all things that can and should be addressed with people we love and trust. This kind of godly dissatisfaction can motivate us toward making godly changes that honor and glorify God more.

But the kind of complaining we need to be desperately aware and deeply repentant of is the kind that accuses God of not giving us the things we think we deserve to have. It's the kind of complaining the Israelites did when they left Egypt on their way to the Promised Land. They didn't believe that God really had a great exit plan and that He would be faithful to provide exactly what they needed for their survival, health and future. So they grumbled. Anytime their level of comfort was being challenged, they questioned God and challenged Moses by asking him why their deliverance felt more like death in the wilderness. It was a lack of faith that led to their verbal discontent, and the root of it was unbelief. They simply didn't believe that God was going to deliver on His promises. Their vision of God was obscured because their eyes were facing inward rather than upward.

Maybe this describes you. As you've read the pages of this book, maybe the Holy Spirit has convicted you of this same pattern of ungodly complaining that we looked at in the children of Israel and in the prophet Jonah. Maybe you're shocked to see how ingrained it's become in you and how deeply it informs your thoughts, conversations and even prayers.

So let's talk about some practical ways that complaining affects us and affects others, and about what kind of godly disciplines we can apply to help combat our glut of grumbling so that the fruit of gratefulness may emerge instead.

With that said, let me make a caveat here. Even more important than applying godly disciplines to our lives is applying God's grace to them first and foremost. For the Christian, Christ's death on the cross means that all of our sins, including grumbling and complaining, have been crucified with Him. This grace that saved us is also the grace that sustains us, so we always want to be careful not to let good and godly disciplines become the god we think is saving and sanctifying us.

Grace anticipates and allows for our shortcomings. This is good news because it means that God is never surprised by our sin, and He doesn't love us any less when we do sin. What's important is that we're actually engaged in the struggle against our sin! That our hearts are soft and open to the Spirit as He conforms us more deeply into the image of Christ by revealing areas of sin in our lives that need crucifying.

How Complaining Affects Us

Since I brought up the subject of travel earlier, let me take the opportunity to say that I absolutely abhor delayed flights. For some reason, there are few things that cause my complaint meter to go through the red than when I have to spend any extra time waiting in an airport terminal. Part of my frustration is that I like to be on time, which is a trait I probably inherited from my dad, who was an ex-Navy man and a stickler for punctuality. His legendary line that lives on in infamy (in our family, at least) was "If you're a minute late, you might as well be an hour late, because late is late." Now I've never taken it that far (sorry, Pops), but I do know that being late can be the cause of stress in my life, and delayed flights seem to be one of those things that compound that stress. There is one particular flight I took some years back that really sticks out in my mind as a painful but sanctifying experience.

My wife and I were on our way from California to Ohio, with a layover in Phoenix. Everything was right on schedule until an hour before takeoff in Phoenix, when we were informed that our flight would be delayed indefinitely. Now I'd experienced many delayed flights in the past but for some reason I became unglued over this one. It might have been because I was flying out for a job interview! At any rate, my saintly wife tried to calm me down as we found some seats to settle into. Right as we sat down, a kind, elderly man who worked in the terminal came over and started chatting with us about where we were heading and I just unloaded all of my anger and complaints on him. I knew it wasn't his fault and I even said as much, but I wanted to vent and he was the moving target.

My wife was aghast, but the man listened, smiled and kept his good humor before asking me what we were heading to Ohio for. I told him it was for a job interview. "Oh yeah? What's the job?" It was then that my blood ran cold. I thought about making something up, but I knew I'd been exposed. I could barely look at him as I mumbled, "Well, it's for a pastor position at a church." He seemed unfazed and proceeded to carry on chatting to us about this and that. I'll never know what he thought in the moment or if he thought anything at all, but the incident humbled me to my core. I later went to him and apologized for my ungodly, undignified rant.

Complaining affects us. It shames us. It exposes us. It humbles us. It reveals the hardness of our hearts. It narrows our focus to rest only on ourselves. It blinds us to who God is and to what our true needs are. What it did in the airport was expose my heart and hinder my witness to somebody who may not have known Christ. In His mercy, God gave me grace to confess my sin and repent to this man before our flight departed.

Despite my sinful struggles in this area, God has used stories like this in my life to remind me of how close my heart is to my tongue and why I need to be careful, as Solomon instructs us in Proverbs, to "keep your heart with all vigilance, for from it flow the springs of life" (4:23). Complaining lowers that guard of safekeeping and allows the springs that flow from our heart to become bitter and poisonous fountains.

Here are just three ways that complaining affects us (and there are surely more than these):

It produces hard hearts.

Constant complaining contributes to the wear and tear of our hearts in a way that produces a hardness in them. It can be compared in some ways to how you use the brakes on your automobile. You want to make sure that the only time you put your foot on the brakes is when you need to either slow down or come to a complete stop. If you keep your foot perpetually resting on the brakes, you're going to quickly burn through your brake pads and experience the metal-on-metal squeal of your rotors grinding against the place your brake pads used to be. Complaining is like that deafening squeal, where underneath the clatter is a heart rubbing against distrust and unbelief.

In speaking to the church at Ephesus, the apostle Paul says that those who have received new life in Christ should not be living as those still enslaved to their old life.

> Now this I say and testify in the Lord, that you must no longer walk as the Gentiles do, in the futility of their minds. They are darkened in their understanding, alienated from the life of God because of the ignorance that is in them, due to their hardness of heart. They have become callous and have given themselves up to sensuality, greedy to practice every kind of impurity. (Eph. 4:17–19)

According to Paul, before Christ saved us our hearts were hardened due to our ignorance of Him, and not only that, they were calloused, meaning they were impenetrable and unable to even see the light of Christ until the Holy Spirit shattered the darkness that blinded us.

Complaining brings us back to walking in our old Gentile life, instead of living out our new gospel life, letting "no corrupting talk come out of your mouths, but only such as is good for building up, as fits the occasion, that it may give grace to those who hear" (4:29). Grumbling is an action of the heart and mind that goes resolutely against the truth of God's grace to produce a brittle hardness in our hearts. This hardness has to continually be broken through the "heartbreaking" work of the Holy Spirit.

It causes blindness.

Complaining also blinds us to the definitive reality of God's grace in our lives—to who God is, how He's worked for us in the past and how He continues to work through us into the future. It blinds us to the hope we have that "he who began a good work in you will bring it to completion at the day of Jesus Christ" (Phil. 1:6).

If God is faithful to complete the good work He began in us, complaining is a way that we prove ourselves blind, ignorant and unbelieving of this gracious truth. It's the act of returning to the darkness we once lived in rather than the light that now lives in us. "For at one time you were darkness, but now you are light in the Lord. Walk as children of light (for the fruit of light is found in all that is good and right and true), and try to discern what is pleasing to the Lord. Take no part in the unfruitful works of darkness, but instead expose them" (Eph. 5:8–11).

Instead of complaining about the things we aren't trusting God for, we can counteract that by spending our time discerning what is pleasing to the Lord. We "give thanks, for your name is near. We recount your wondrous deeds" (Ps. 75:1). Blindness is forgetfulness. It's like a parent having to remind their spoiled, oblivious child of all the kind things they do for them on a daily basis. The clothes they wear, the food they eat, the toys they play with and the house they live in are the result of a father and mother who sacrifice their lives to love, nurture and care for them.

John Piper, in his book *Don't Waste Your Life* says "The really wonderful moments of joy in this world are not the moments of self-satisfaction, but self-forgetfulness. Standing on the edge of the Grand Canyon and contemplating your own greatness is pathological. At such moments we are made for a magnificent joy that comes from outside ourselves."[1] It's this "blindness" to oneself that actually opens our eyes to the goodness and glory of God.

It gives us a higher view of self.

Complaining creates wrong thinking. It gives us a higher view of self and in turn gives us a lower view of God. This creates self-consumers in all of us. It illustrates the faulty thinking that says I know what's better for me than God, and what's better for me will always be the thing that's most comfortable to me. It keeps us groping after earthly treasures instead of laying up for ourselves "treasures in heaven, where neither moth nor rust destroys and where thieves do not break in and steal" (Matt. 6:20).

Whenever I find myself complaining against the unrealized pursuit of something I feel I have the right to attain, what I'm ultimately saying is that I know better than God. The blueprints that I've drafted for my life and my future take precedence over what God has designed for me.

The result is pride and stubbornness and a refusal to submit to God's more humble desires and designs for our lives. In reality, grumbling turns us into glory hogs, rather than people whom the gospel humbles toward caring more for the needs of others. Tim Keller writes, "The thing we would remember from meeting a truly gospel-humble person is how much they seemed to be totally interested in us. Because the essence of gospel-humility is not thinking more of myself or thinking less of myself, it is thinking of myself less."[2]

How Complaining Affects Others

One of the marks of maturity for the Christian is that we begin to see our sin as being much less narrow and insignificant than we originally thought. We see it as not just affecting us, but spreading like an infection to others because nobody is immune to the widespread damage that sin causes. The apostle Paul goes to great lengths to inform us that the church is not made up of a series of autonomous human beings, but that "There is one body and one Spirit—just as you were called to the one hope that belongs to your call—one Lord, one faith, one baptism, one God and Father of all, who is over all and through all and in all" (Eph. 4:4–6).

What this tells us is that the church is a community of believers knit together with one Holy Spirit holding us in gospel-infused harmony. Because of this, "If one member suffers, all suffer together; if one member is honored, all rejoice together" (1 Cor. 12:26). So with this understanding in place, we live with the sobering truth that our ungodly complaining can have a widespread, negative effect on our brothers and sisters in the faith.

Paul says, instead of being immature children who are unstable, easily tempted and deceived by human cunning, "Rather, speaking the truth in love, we are to grow up in every way into him who is the head, into Christ, from whom the whole body, joined and held together by every joint with which it is equipped, when each part is working properly, makes the body grow so that it builds itself up in love" (Eph. 4:15–16). When grumbling and complaining reach their zenith, they represent parts that aren't working properly. People are not being built up in love, but rather are torn down by a profound lack of it. Here are two ways that complaining affects others:

It Tempts Others To Sin.

Complaining tempts others to complain. The addictive quality of complaining is so potent that when we're in the company of complainers we're usually chomping at the bit to share our own tales of intolerance. The problem with this is that Scripture comes down fairly heavily against tempting other people to sin. "Therefore let us not pass judgment on one another any longer, but rather decide never to put a stumbling block or hindrance in the way of a brother" (Rom. 14:13). Our heart for our neighbor should be one that never wants to give any opportunity to see them stumble and fall.

> Therefore, having put away falsehood, let each one of you speak the truth with his neighbor, for we are members one of another. Be angry and do not sin; do not let the sun go down on your anger, and give no opportunity to the devil. (Eph. 4:25–27)

Complaining gives an opportunity for the devil to use our words to tempt others to become angry and discontent.

Paul once again admonishes us to "Let your speech always be gracious, seasoned with salt, so that you may know how you ought to answer each person" (Col. 4:6).

It Invites Others to Doubt God's Grace.

It's a morning I'll never forget. My wife and I were sitting quietly across from one another having our devotional time when I heard her exclaim, "Oh no . . . " I could tell from her tone that it wasn't good. Some dear friends of ours who were pregnant with their second child contacted us to let us know they'd gone to the hospital that morning because they were experiencing some early signs of labor. We'd been anticipating this moment, as the baby was only one week away from delivery. Instead, they wrote to tell us that their daughter's heart had stopped beating. In a moment, she was gone.

Funeral preparations were made for the following week and on Tuesday morning, we gathered at the funeral home to conduct the service. What we saw that day during calling hours was something my wife and I still talk about often. Our friends stood at the front of the room near their baby as a line of people formed to offer their condolences. With each passing face, our friends graciously offered their tears, hugs and some occasional laughs to assure everyone that this was not a hopeless situation but that God was lovingly in control.

It dawned on us that it wasn't our friends who were being comforted as much as it was they who were offering comfort to everyone else. In that moment, God was doing a work in their hearts that went far beyond the despair that was no doubt seeking to crush them. It's interesting to think that if anyone had the right to complain in that moment, it was them! The temptation to shake their fists at God was surely there, but there would be none of that. They chose to use this brief moment in time to hold the hands of others and comfort them in their own grief and mourning.

It was a story that swept through our small town. "Heartbroken but not hopeless" was the banner our friends used over and over again to draw people to the truth that it's only the gospel that has any power to provide true and effective hope.

What our friends did was invite people to see God at work in what many would describe as an unworkable situation. Far from causing people to doubt God's grace, they used the tragedy of their daughter's death as an occasion for our community to see what this grace looks like when God's people are faced with the unimaginable. To see that, although we live in a fallen world that is broken by the pain of sin and death, because of the gospel none of it is final.

When we publicly shake our fists and raise our complaints before God, we invite others to doubt the effectiveness of God's grace, grace that satisfies our past, sustains our present and seals our future. Jonathan Edwards writes in *Religious Affections*, "Grace is the seed of glory, the dawning of glory in the heart, and therefore grace is the earnest of the future inheritance."[3] Knowing this, we should tremble at the thought of letting any word or deed become the occasion for another to doubt the sufficiency of God's grace for every aspect of our lives.

Is There Ever A Time To Complain?

Are there ever good and godly reasons for complaining? It isn't always spitting out uncontrolled mountains of malcontent, is it? Aren't there many times when our complaints are valid, and we share them not to tempt others to sin, but for others to pray? Isn't complaining sometimes the way that we plead before God like David does in Psalms when he cries,

> How long, O Lord? Will you forget me forever? How long will you hide your face from me? How long must I take counsel in my soul and have sorrow in my heart all the day? How long shall my enemy be exalted over me? Consider and answer me, O Lord my God; light up my eyes, lest I sleep the sleep of death, lest my enemy say, "I have prevailed over him," lest my foes rejoice because I am shaken. (13:1–4)

David is being bold here, isn't he? He's complaining honestly before the Lord with words that sound like he's almost demanding that God answer him and reveal to him how He's going to intervene in his life.

What this illustrates to us is the grace and mercy of God and how He allows us to come honestly before Him with our questions and concerns because He understands the trials, difficulties and uncertainties that we face. This is the kind of complaining to God that exposes our brokenness before Him and pleads honestly for help and hope in the midst of our despair. It's this kind of honesty before the Lord that leads us to hopefulness in Him. David finishes his pleading by singing, "But I have trusted in your steadfast love; my heart shall rejoice in your salvation. I will sing to the Lord, because he has dealt bountifully with me" (Ps. 13:5–6). Our pleading before God should eventually lead to praising Him as we remember all the ways He lovingly provides for us.

Then what about complaining to others? Do we always tempt others to sin when we complain, or do our complaints sometimes serve as a plea for wisdom and prayer? How do we discern between the two?

Here's the thing: we should speak honestly with one another, and often. There are times when we need to share things in our lives that are not going well in hopes of receiving equipping, encouragement and prayer. This is how others bear our burdens and walk alongside of us through the valleys. This is what God calls the church body to do for one another. Galatians tells us to "Bear one another's burdens, and so fulfill the law of Christ" (6:2). The law of Christ meaning, "You shall love the Lord your God with all your heart and with all your soul and with all your strength and with all your mind, and your neighbor as yourself" (Luke 10:27).

So the question for us when we're sharing our burdens and complaints with others should be this: are we inviting them to join in, or to join us in prayer? Are we inviting them to validate our dissatisfactions or to remind us of the truth of the gospel?

Remember, Hebrews 10:24 says, "And let us consider how to stir up one another to love and good works."

So before another word comes out, consider the consequences it might have on your hearer. In this way we will fulfill the law of Christ.

Reflection Questions

1. Recall some of the ways in which complaining has had an adverse effect on you. Do you see how it's produced hard-heartedness, blindness and a higher view of self?

2. How do you think your complaining has affected others? Do you see evidence of how it may have tempted others to sin and to doubt God's grace in their lives?

3. What does our complaining ultimately say about our love for God? For others?

8

ABSTAINING FROM COMPLAINING

"For I do not do the good I want, but the evil I do not want
is what I keep on doing."

Romans 7:19

We deny that good works have any share in justification, but we
claim full authority for them in the lives of the righteous.

—John Calvin

S o let's get practical. How on earth do we stop complaining?
Because of our natural pull toward self-sufficiency, we have to
guard against the tendency to grit our teeth and get it done.

As we discussed previously, the gospel has already gotten it
done. The beauty of grace is that God loves us before, during
and after we stumble and fall, so we work joyously under the
completed work of Christ.

With that said, here are three practical things to consider
when we are convicted of our complaining.

Pause

Whenever God reveals a pattern of sin in our lives, it's good
to pause and let ourselves humbly receive the truth of it. Hopefully you've had some moments of contemplation and conviction

while reading this book, which should lead you to spend some time taking stock of your speech patterns. Are you someone who regularly falls into a pattern of grumbling and complaining? Recall some recent conversations you've had with family, with friends, with coworkers and with God. Can you trace the fruit of your expression? Does it build up or tear down? Does it encourage or embitter? Does it offer hope or heartlessness? Does it communicate grace or condemnation? Does it express grumbling or gratefulness?

If what the Bible says is true, that "out of the abundance of the heart the mouth speaks" (Matt. 12:34), then take the time to closely examine what's feeding your heart and affecting the outflow of your mouth.

Being a California native, this thing called "winter in Ohio" has been a somewhat new experience for me. Winter in Southern California consists of some occasional rain, sixty-degree days and trees changing colors. Throw on a hoodie, say "Merry Christmas" and it passes into spring faster than you count to three. Ohio has *real* winter. For three to four months, it's cold and snowy. People tend to hibernate inside. My wife likes to bake and the pounds like to pile on. How much food I intake during the winter really affects the amount of energy I'm able to expend when spring finally arrives. I have to be careful about what I eat in the winter because the truth will be exposed in the spring.

I've never regretted any of the times I've silenced my inner defense attorney after being confronted with some hard truth about sinful patterns that have emerged in my life. It's not easy to receive criticism, but it's much more damaging to continue to run from the conviction that comes from good counsel. I don't have a good enough memory to recount all the times my wife has been gracious enough to call me out on certain things, but I do know that I benefit greatly in those moments when I pause to listen to her.

Pray

Did you have a feeling I would mention prayer? It's interesting that out of all the things we're asked to do in Scripture, prayer is the one that requires the least amount of physical exertion and yet seems to be the thing we do the least. Speaking of spiritual warfare, Paul admonishes the Ephesians to be "praying at all times in the Spirit, with all prayer and supplication. To that end keep alert with all perseverance, making supplication for all the saints" (Eph. 6:18). Complaining is a spiritual issue, requiring spiritual warfare to combat it. Our best artillery for battle is having an ongoing conversation with God, asking Him to protect us, keep us alert, give us endurance and then praying that He would equip our fellow brothers and sisters in Christ in the same way so that we don't tempt one another to complain.

We wrongly think of prayer as something we do in hopes of changing God's mind, but in reality, we pray because it changes our minds. In the play *Shadowlands*, William Nicholson distills C.S. Lewis' thinking on the subject in the famous line, "I pray because I can't help myself. I pray because I'm helpless. I pray because the need flows out of me all the time, waking and sleeping. It doesn't change God. it changes me."[1]

Every time we pray, it's like being reintroduced to the glory of God. God's glory reminds us of our own depravity, and our own depravity reminds us how much we need Him and how much He loves us. So how then should we pray?

First off, confess to the Lord that you even have a problem with complaining at all. For many of us, this is not the kind of sin that will carry as much weight as other sins in our lives that we consider much more overt and damaging. And yet we've seen how greatly it displeases God when His people are not thankful to Him.

Second, if this still feels shrug-worthy to you, pray that the Holy Spirit would convict you of your apathy and give you a greater sensitivity to the subtlety of this sin.

Third, pray that God would guard you against the temptation to complain. As we pointed out earlier, complaining can be an incredibly enjoyable activity that fuels our sinful sense of entitlement and victimization, which can be easily validated when in the company of others.

One of the evidences of the Spirit's sanctification in our lives is that we have an ever-increasing love for what God loves as well as a hatred of what God hates. We should hate complaining as much as God hates it, because it doesn't glorify Him. Our prayer should be like David's when he said, "Create in me a clean heart, O God, and renew a right spirit within me" (Ps. 51:10).

A spirit of complaining is not the clean heart or right spirit that God desires for His sons and daughters.

Here is a sample prayer of repentance for our complaining:

Gracious and Loving God,

Thank You that because of Jesus Christ, I'm able to come to You with boldness and without fear of punishment, anger or even surprise at the sin I lay before Your throne. I confess that although You have given me an overabundance of good things, my heart is often blinded by entitlement and ungratefulness. I so easily forget the loving-kindness, undeserved grace and daily mercies that You give me without reserve. Help me to take this sin of complaining as seriously as I take other sins about which I feel far more greatly convicted than this one. Guard me from being taken in by the comforting allure that complaining provides and the false but addicting assurance it implants in my heart. Let my comfort rest in the all-satisfying joy of Your eternal salvation that doesn't disappoint or diminish in this life or in the age to come.

In the name of Jesus Christ, our hope and glory, Amen.

Pursue Gratefulness

Many times, solutions are simple. When I visit my dentist, he doesn't typically send me home with a manual on advanced dentistry so I can better care for my teeth. Instead, he gently reinforces the importance of two basic practices for having healthy teeth and gums: brushing and flossing. If I consistently practice those two things and come in for regular cleanings, I'll avoid all kinds of dental unpleasantries such as cavities, root canals, gum disease and dentures. The problem is, I don't pursue those two things as well as I should. I don't always brush my teeth before going to bed at night, and my flossing would probably be on par with how often I've sprouted wings and learned how to fly. Because of that, I've struggled with minor dental issues for most of my life.

The same is true in the area of complaining. The only way to combat complaining is for God to replace our grumbling hearts with grateful ones. And that's it. That's it? All of this and that's the big conclusion? It really is! To go from grumbling to gratefulness means that something has to happen in us to change what comes out of us.

Proverbs says, "The way of the wicked is an abomination to the Lord, but he loves him who pursues righteousness" (15:9).

To his protégé Timothy, the apostle Paul wrote, "But as for you, O man of God, flee these things. Pursue righteousness, godliness, faith, love, steadfastness, gentleness" (1 Tim. 6:11).

Although it feels like complaining tends to pour out of us unaware, it's actually a choice we make every time we open our mouths. To combat it means that we pursue the act of being grateful instead. It's literally the act of pursuing the righteousness of God rather than the validation of man. Of pursuing godliness rather than worldliness. Of pursuing faith in God rather than the fiction of the world. Of pursuing the love of God over the praise of men. Of pursuing steadfastness rather than whatever satisfies in the moment. Of pursuing gentleness rather than the critical spirit that characterizes complaining.

Instead of complaining, we pursue Christ, who suffered on the cross and forgave His enemies, never uttering a complaint, but enduring to the end for the joy that was set before Him.

NOTES

CHAPTER 1

1. *Oxford Dictionaries*, s.v. "complain," accessed June 23, 2015,. http://www.oxforddictionaries.com/us/definition/american_english/complain

CHAPTER 2

1. C.S. Lewis, *The Weight of Glory* (London: Macmillan, 1949), 3-4.

2. J.C. Ryle, *Holiness* (London: James Clarke & Co., 1952), accessed June 23, 2015, http://www.ccel.org/ccel/ryle/holiness.iii.iii.html

CHAPTER 4

1. John Piper, *When I Don't Desire God* (Wheaton: Crossway, 2004), 33.

CHAPTER 5

1. *Merriam-Webster Dictionary*, s.v. "happiness," accessed June 23, 2015, http://www.merriam-webster.com/dictionary/happiness

2. Blaise Pascal, *Pensées* (Oxford: Oxford University Press, 1995), 65.

3. John Piper, *For Your Joy* (Minneapolis: Desiring God, 2005), 39.

4. *Merriam-Webster Dictionary*, s.v. "joy," accessed June 23, 2015, http://www.merriam-webster.com/dictionary/joy

5. Tim Keller, *Counterfeit Gods* (New York: Dutton, 2009), xiv.

6. C.S. Lewis, *Mere Christianity* (New York: Harper Collins, 1952), 134.

7. Dietrich Bonhoeffer, *The Cost of Discipleship* (London: SCM Press, 1959), 87.

8. John Krakauer, *Into the Wild* (London: Macmillan, 2011), 155.

9. Tullian Tchividjian, *Jesus + Nothing = Everything* (Wheaton: Crossway, 2011), 52.

CHAPTER 6

1. *Merriam-Webster Dictionary*, s.v. "undeserved," accessed June 23, 2015, http://www.merriam-webster.com/dictionary/undeserved

2. *Merriam-Webster Dictionary*, s.v. "grace," accessed June 23, 2015, http://www.merriam-webster.com/dictionary/grace

3. *Merriam-Webster Dictionary*, s.v. "grateful," accessed June 23, 2015, http://www.merriam-webster.com/dictionary/grateful

CHAPTER 7

1. John Piper, *Don't Waste Your Life* (Wheaton: Crossway, 2003), 33-34.

2. Tim Keller, *The Freedom of Self-Forgetfulness* (Chorley, England: 10Publishing, 2012), 31-32.

3. Jonathan Edwards, *Religious Affections* (New Haven: Yale University Press, 1959), 236.

CHAPTER 8

1. William Nicholson, *Shadowlands* (New York: Samuel French, Inc., 1990), 81.

PUBLICATIONS

Fort Washington, PA 19034

This book is published by CLC Publications, an outreach of CLC
Ministries International. The purpose of CLC is to make evangelical
Christian literature available to all nations so that people may come
to faith and maturity in the Lord Jesus Christ. We hope this book has
been life changing and has enriched your walk with God through the
work of the Holy Spirit. If you would like to know more about CLC,
we invite you to visit our website:

www.clcusa.org

To know more about the remarkable story of the founding of
CLC International we encourage you to read

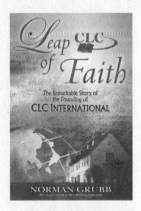

LEAP OF FAITH

Norman Grubb

Paperback
Size 5¹/₄ x 8, Pages 248
ISBN: 978-0-87508-650-7
ISBN (*e-book*): 978-1-61958-055-8